The Secret
of the Seventh Arc

The Secret
of the Seventh Arc

The story about the disappearance
of the Malaysia flight MH370

Edited by:

Stanisław Bednarz

Miloš Jesenský

Robert Leśniakiewicz

PAPERBACK ISBN: 978-1-7363485-5-0

EPUB ISBN: 978-1-3930430-9-6

***

WRITTEN BY STANISLAW BEDNARZ, ROBERT KONSTANTY LEŚNIAKIEWICZ

& DR MILOŠ JESENSKÝ

PUBLISHED BY ROYAL HAWAIIAN PRESS

COVER ART BY TYRONE ROSHANTHA

TRANSLATED BY SZYMON NOWAK

PUBLISHING ASSISTANCE: DOROTA RESZKE

***

FOR MORE WORKS BY THIS AUTHOR, PLEASE VISIT:

WWW.ROYALHAWAIIANPRESS.COM

***

VERSION NUMBER 1.00

INTRODUCTION

It is a puzzle in which all the elements are clear and transparent, but together they form an opaque whole. These words were written by Stanisław Lem in his cult sensational novel "Katar" and they can serve as a motto for this study, which we wrote to show the reader what dark and opaque matter we deal with.

For this is an extraordinary case! A huge flying machine measuring 60 x 64 m and weighing 300 tons disappears without a trace in the gloom of the Malayan night! Six years of searching are still fruitless, and there is even no fixed site of a possible catastrophe! And seemingly, all this took place in a world where satellites and sensors can hear a mouse sneeze from thousands of kilometers away... - and despite all this, the waters of the Indian Ocean or any other sea have closed forever over MH-370. After all, we don't even know where the plane flew after the pilots turned off its transponder!

One can only make assumptions and hypotheses. For us, it is incomprehensible as all this happened in an area bristling with radar stations and other air traffic detection devices. And nobody has seen anything, nobody knows anything, like in a Czech comedy. In the waters of increased sea traffic - hundreds of ships pass daily. And yet no one knows anything...

We wanted to present to the reader the development of the situation as well as new searches and hopes for finding the missing people and machine. Some are factual, some are quite fantastic. And here they are...

Stanisław Bednarz
Miloš Jesenský
Robert Leśniakiewicz

Chapter 1

The missing

They also stated that all the aircraft's flight monitoring systems couldn't be destroyed simultaneously and immediately. This model of the Boeing 777 is one of the most modern passenger aircraft, it couldn't fall from the sky without a trace, and its range is 7,250 miles/11,600 km. If we had a FF[1] case, it

---

[1] Friedly fire - shooting down of the plane by own or allied air defense units. Events like that have happened many times, such as the shooting down of the Iranian Airbus A300B2-203, side number EP-IBU, flight IR-655, by the American anti-aircraft cruiser USS Vincennes in the Persian Gulf on July 3, 1988, at 10:17 am IRST.

would have had to be detected by satellites constantly observing the Earth.[2]

Some speculate that the plane and passengers were safe and sustained no damage but were elsewhere and we will soon know where. We can deal here with the advanced capabilities of the Aliens, or with military super-tech equipment - which no one may know exist, and which are undetectable by conventional methods of technical observation.

Skyjacking by pilots or passengers of that plane is very likely. The commander of this aircraft was known for his negative attitude towards the Malaysian government and may have introduced his hijacking plan as part of the protest.

Meanwhile, **Dr. Ibrahim Wahid** writes:

"More than 50 UFOs were sighted over Phuket, Thailand after flight MH-370 was reported missing - A UFO was seen on the radar as it tripled its speed when passing by the Malaysian plane." (Thanks to Dr. Ibrahim Wahid from Cairo).

1.1 My 2 cents

---

[2] This is not so obvious, because while flying over many regions of the Earth, the reconnaissance satellites are simply turned off to save batteries and observation equipment.

That's what George Filer says. Indeed, the case is very mysterious and the search for the plane that has been missing for two weeks still attracts media attention. After all, such a powerful machine as the Boeing 777 is not a needle and it had to be somewhere. The problem is that the Indian Ocean is a huge expanse of water, and to search it even with the most modern and sophisticated techniques, is not as easy as it seems.

A week ago, I approached some familiar ufologists, journalists and writers for their opinion on this subject, and here is what they said to me:

Albert Rosales (USA) "I think something should be found, some wreckage, whatever, and it's weird there are no traces. And if it wasn't skyjacked to North Korea or another hostile country, maybe it is at Putin's dacha? Whether for political reasons - it's hard to say. Now the radars are said to have picked up three drifting objects in the area where the plane disappeared."[3]

Dr Jiři Kult (Czech Republic) "The case is very interesting, there is no evidence of a plane crash, and the hypothesis about some terrorists hijacking the plane is very possible. However, I believe a seizure by ET may be more likely. We will see!"

Dr. Mikhail Gerstein (Russia) "I am of the opinion that it was an ordinary disaster. Please see satellite photos on the

---

[3] In the Gulf of Thailand.

website - http://www.extremetech.com/extreme/178156-the-mystery-of-flight-mh370-how-can-we-track-a-smartphone-anywhere-on-earth- but-a-giant-plane-can-go-missing - all debris was scattered at sea and sunk. The sea is able to hide even larger objects than such an ordinary Boeing, and without a trace."

My opinion: Personally, I think it was a skyjacking. A flight in the multi-ton machine at an altitude of 100-200 m above the ocean is very risky - the plane is not a ground effect vehicle. Boeing is definitely somewhere at the bottom of the ocean, and people? Well - the sharks had an all-you-can-eat buffet... (R.K.F. Leśniakiewicz).

And, of course, the Great Conspiracy Theory:

IvIartyn Pe (Poland) - 777 has so far parked somewhere on the dark side of the moon and waits like a crouching tiger and a hidden dragon... It is impossible that the signal of such a large aluminum plane disappeared from civilian and military radar screens, with the transponder switched off - there was no such possibility! Therefore, I am inclined to the version that the plane of flight MH370 with 239 passengers on board has been taken over by a plane with the AWACS system of the American aviation and in the near future it may be used for another plane bomb attack with the use of nuclear weapons in a new false flag operation.

Skyjacking... yes, that's right...! but without sharks and let's not sweep everything under the rug [...] the film escape at an altitude of 100-200 m above the ocean to avoid being targeted by the radar beam is a Stone Age archaism... This disappearance occurred at an altitude of 29,500 ft/~ 9,830 m, so explaining that it was too low for radar detection is pointless... AWACS could disrupt or completely intercept the reflection signal from civilian and military radars, which was so weak that the plane disappeared for them... Besides, let's not forget that on board there were owners of patents worth billions of dollars... If you believe a person like Jim Stone by an accidental accident caused by accident a few days before the ill-fated flight from Kuala Lumpur, the US Patent Office received an application for patent protection of a technology allowing to achieve "invisibility"... this is just an irrelevant leg of this topic... In my opinion it is the beginning of a chain of a multi-threaded case in the history of aviation with a disturbingly large number of symbols causing chaos...

Could it be so? Until the plane or its wreckage is found, we can only speculate and come up with various theories and hypotheses. I can say with a clear conscience - "I know that I don't know anything." I hope to find out the truth about the flight MH370 of the Boeing 777. But when ...?[4]

---

[4] Compiled by - R.K.F. Leśniakiewicz

George A. Filer III (MUFON)

Chapter 2

Strange phenomena at the seaside

What happened to the Malaysia Airlines Boeing 777, flight MH-370, with the serial number 9M-MRO, flying from Kuala Lumpur (KUL) to Beijing (PEK). There were 239 people on board, including 12 crew members.

The plane took off on March 8, 2014 at 00:41AM MYT and headed north-northeast over the Gulf of Thailand (Siamese) towards the coast of Vietnam. Landing was scheduled for 06:30AM CST. However, the plane didn't reach it - at 01:22AM MYT the navigation and communication systems stopped working - the plane disappeared from the radar screens. Only the transmitters sending signals to the satellites were working - every hour and the last signal was sent by the engines at 08:41AM MYT. This means that the plane could still be in the air 51 minutes after 08:41AM, meaning the engines had to stop functioning by 09:30AM MYT. According to unconfirmed information, the Malaysian military radars were still tracking an unidentified object that could be the missing Boeing at around 2:40AM, i.e. more than an hour after the disappearance of MH-370 from civilian radars. It was headed west, towards the Indian Ocean. According to sources from The New York Times, the object first climbed to 45,000 ft/~ 15,000 m, then descended to 23,000 ft/~ 7,667 m.

The Malaysian authorities have established two search strips based on satellite data but also thanks to flight MH370 simulation. Within a week, using an identical Boeing 777-200ER, the search teams made a flight consistent with the known information about the MH370.

As The New York Times reminds, the northern part of the search strip is a heavily militarized area, including China (also Tibet), Afghanistan, Pakistan, Central Asian republics and Iran.

Data analysts from the New York medium WNYC calculated that there were as many as 634 airports in 26 countries within the range of the aircraft, where it could theoretically land.

Although combustion depends, among others on the altitude and the speed of the aircraft, analysts estimate that when the last

---

ping was sent at 08:11AM MYT, there must have already been very little kerosene[5] in the fuel tanks of the Boeing 777.

All sources agree that the circumstantial evidence indicates that the disappearance of the plane is the result of the actions of a person trained in pilotage and familiar with this type of plane. Suspicions fell among others on the Captain of MH370, Zaharie Ahmad Shah, whose home was searched yesterday. He had in his house, among others, a very advanced flight simulator. Authorities also searched the home of the first mate and rechecked all passengers.

In accordance with international aviation law, the investigation should be carried out by the country in which the accident occurred. For the MH370 flight, multilateral activities are coordinated by Malaysia, where the plane took off from, and where it was registered. However, international cooperation and the lack of data make it difficult to search efficiently. Malaysia has been criticized for its lack of transparency, and the Chinese news agency Xinhua released yesterday a harsh assessment of the exploration action. Only yesterday, after more than a week of searching, the Prime Minister of Malaysia for the first time summed up the information at a press conference.[6]

---

[5] Aviation kerosene used as fuel for jet engines.

[6] Dominik Sipiński http://www.pasazer.com/in-16033-minal,tydzien,co,wiemy,o,mh370.php

What happened? There are basically three main hypotheses:

1. The plane crashed into the sea for unknown reasons, leaving no traces of the crash;

2. The plane was skyjacked by two terrorists with stolen Italian and Austrian passports;

3. The plane was hijacked by the crew in an unknown direction and for unknown reasons - possibly political.

We can already reject points 2 and 3 - if it was about a ransom or political demands of terrorists, they would have been known within 72 hours. There was no such thing... Therefore only the catastrophe remained.

Of course, there are also extraordinary hypotheses about the Spacemen hijacking the plane and people - just as it was with many planes and ships over and in the waters of the Bermuda Triangle.

Such hypotheses are probable because the plane flew in the air corridor over the Gulf of Thailand (Siamese), where - as many authors say - mysterious luminous circles had appeared on and in the water, as well as UFOs and USOs were observed. **Aleksander Grobicki** writes:

The first news that made these luminous circles famous was the testimony of a credible witness published on June 30, 1870 in the "Kölnische Zeitung". They were to emerge from the depths of the Indian Ocean and surround the ship with glowing mist, making the night day.

More precise was the report by Captain Evans, a hydrographer and member of the Royal Society, given in 1879 to the British Admiralty, recalled in 1977 by the French monthly "Science et Vie" in an article entitled "Strange phenomena waiting to be explained":

The deck of the Vulture ship crossing the Gulf of Siamese. 10 p.m. Dark night. Starry sky. We are surrounded by strange light circles. The observer climbed the mast and found that the rays were coming out of the sea. They have the nature of very fast vibrations. On the port side, it resembles a wheel with spokes made of light rays. On the starboard, it seems to be rotating in the opposite direction. The observer as a scientist has thus concluded that this was only an illusion, since they were actually parallel circles of light. Each was 8 m wide, the gap between them was 25 m, and the speed with which they were moving was about 130 km/h... [...]

On July 24, 1908, George A. Turner, the second officer of the SS Conseller, witnessed how his ship suddenly found itself in the range of rays of extraordinary phosphorescence in the Gulf of Siamese, 200 to 300 meters long and 30 meters wide.[7]

Other facts are quoted by **Arnold Mostowicz:**

---

[7] Here and further Aleksander Grobicki – "Nie tylko Trójkąt Bermudzki", Gdansk 1980.

...this was the case with the Portuguese brig Santa Maria, where in 1884 all its sailors were found dead. So it was also with the ship Abbey S. Hart, on board of which the corpses of sailors and a dying captain were found. There also - in the Gulf of Siamese - it disappeared - yes, it disappeared! - during the Indian-Pakistani conflict in 1971, the entire frigate and its crew, and it was found that no submarines were in the vicinity. There, finally, the SS Holchu disappeared without a trace.[8]

The second suspicious body of water is the Strait of Malacca - an area with an equally nasty reputation where UFOs and USOs have been observed in addition to light circles in, on and above the water, as well as luminous circles on and in the water. Aleksander Grobicki described it as follows:

In June 1909, Captain Gabe, the skipper of the Bintang ship sailing through the Strait of Malacca, noticed moving circles of light on the surface of the water. Gabe stated that [...] these light wheels couldn't have had any source other than the depths of the sea.

There have also been cases of mysterious sea disasters in this reservoir. Arnold Mostowicz writes about them:

...it could have happened in the case of the Dutch steamer SS Urang Medan (according to other sources, SS Orang Medan - R.K.L.), whose entire crew died in 1948 for unknown reasons.

---

[8] Arnold Mostowicz – "My z Kosmosu", Warszawa 1978.

The ship crossed the Strait of Malacca when the sea was completely calm. [...]

And finally, the third body of water - the Andaman Sea, where the lights in and under the water were also observed:

On February 7, 1953, the English merchant ship MS Rance noticed the wandering motor vessel SS Holchu between the Andaman and Nicobar islands. Also in this case it turned out that the crew had disappeared.

As you can see, there is a discrepancy between the descriptions of the discovery of the SS Holchu, but all authors agree on one thing - this mystery has not been solved at all ...

And one more thing - searches with the use of satellites in the waters of south-eastern Indian Ocean are very difficult because there is a trash vortex similar to the one in the Pacific between Hawaii, Alaska and California.[9]

---

[9] This case was described at:
http://wszechocean.blogspot.com/2012/03/wszechocean-stan-kleski-rozumu-1.html
http://wszechocean.blogspot.com/2012/03/wszechocean-stan-kleski-rozumu-2.html
http://wszechocean.blogspot.com/2012/03/wszechocean-stan-kleski-rozumu-3.html
http://wszechocean.blogspot.com/2012/03/wszechocean-kleska-rozumu-4.html
http://wszechocean.blogspot.com/2013/03/negatywne-efekty-fukushimy.html http://wszechocean.blogspot.com/2012/10/podroz-

This issue is developmental and only now can we see how much. So far, the remains of this unfortunate plane have not been found among the garbage floating there. It is indeed like looking for a needle in a haystack ...

My friends write:

Kiyoshi Amamiya (Japan): *This is a very interesting event. There are many points of view represented by intellectuals from different countries. Out of these, the view about the mystery of these people stands out. It seems that the remains that have recently been found in the Indian Ocean will be investigated, but it is not known whether these are the remains of the Malaysian plane. The house of the pilot was searched with strange results (e.g. a flight simulator was found). This is a deep mystery indeed.*

Patrick Moncelet (Singapore): *My opinion? Well - the plane began to burn in the air from the cockpit, and the fire rapidly spread to the passenger compartment before it could be contained. The whole plane caught fire and fell apart (oxygen, aluminum, iron oxide) - like the old Hindenburg airship. Its shards fell into the Sea of China, leaving no traces. There are witnesses who saw the plane on fire at high altitude at the same time. One thing that amazes me is the lack of reaction of the authorities to the reports of these witnesses.*

Indeed - it is very strange ...

uczona-na-hel.html

And one more aspect of this mysterious case, namely - some of my friends see the action of special services in this event, which allegedly hijacked the plane because there were specialists in the field of tactical masking of aircraft on board.

Dorota Dybała (Poland): *What is missing here is the passenger list (nowadays it is an important issue), which was mentioned in part by IvIartyn Pe... and by the way - if his hypothesy is true, a similar operation was supposedly carried out on the Titanic... someone will make some money in this way and surely win something... - and one more thing - since various strange events often happen over this area, for what reasons no one wants to change flight routes? ...is it good for someone?*

Zofia Eleonora Piepiórka (Poland): *Until now, only UFOs had the properties of disappearing from radars, i.e. invisibility... The discovery and patenting of "invisibility" is a great technical progress that has a future in the latest space technologies... So the disappearance of the most modern passenger plane may be skyjacking by UFOs, as well as testing of the latest technology... This is reminiscent of the famous "Philadelphia experiment" about which Robert once wrote... Similar experiments were carried out by the Nazis in the port of Gdynia during WWII ... https://www.facebook.com/photo.php?fbid=481082208681948&s et=a.227800907343414.48977.227797157343789&type=1&theat er*

The photo mentioned by Eleonora is a vulgar photomontage, anyway, the plane with such fuel supply wouldn't have been able to cross the entire Pacific and land in the Brazilian jungle. Similarly, flying the other way would have had to cross the entire Indian Ocean, the African continent and the Atlantic...

However, skyjacking to obtain new technologies - this can also be a motive, especially since as a result of the events in Ukraine, gunpowder could be again smelled in Europe... If what Eleonora and Ivartyn Pe writes are true, then in fact - their version may be true or close to the truth. Someone really wants to return to the Cold War and the bipolar world... So we await results of the search.

Robert Leśniakiewicz

Chapter 3

Initial conspiracy theories

British Wikipedia gave the history of the flight MH370 and its disappearance in the form of a table, which I am presenting below, because it is very interesting and may shed some light on this strange tragedy - on March 24, 2014 in the afternoon, a message was announced that the remains of the plane were found on the southern waters of the Indian Ocean. And here is the table of events:

Time (MYT)	Time (GMT)	Event
00:00-00:41 AM	4:41 PM	Departure from Kuala Lumpur
00:20-01:01 AM	5:01 PM	MH-370 confirms ascent to an altitude of 11,000 m
00:26-01:07 AM	5:07 PM	Last data transmission from ACARS, the crew confirms the altitude of 11,000 m
00:38-01:19 AM	5:19 PM	Last voice contact with Malaysian ATC
00:40-01:21 AM	5:21 PM	Last radar contact (transponder) at position N 06°55 '15" - E 103°34'43"
00:41-01:22 AM	5:22 PM	Transponder and ADS-B have been disabled
00:49-01:30 AM	5:30 PM	Unsuccessful voice contact with another aircraft - muttering, dropouts (faddings)
00:56-01:37 AM	5:37 PM	Half-hour waiting for ACARS transmission - missed
01:30-02:11 AM	6:11 PM	The first of seven ACARS signals transmitted hourly by the Inmasat 3F1 satellite
01:34-02:15 AM	6:15 PM	Last radar contact from a Malaysian military radar station located 320 km NW of Penang
05:49-06:30 AM	10:30 PM	Scheduled arrival in Beijing
07:30-08:11 AM	00:11 AM	Last automatic ACARS signal

		provided by Inmarsat
07:49-08:30 AM	00:30 AM	The plane went missing

In spite of this, the mystery remains a mystery - what made the plane flying north, to suddenly change direction to west and then fly towards Antarctica? We don't know that. Yesterday's "Wiadomości" of TVP1 showed that the remains of the plane were found in the Indian Ocean at the position: S44°57'29" - E090°13'43" - between Australia and the islands of Amsterdam and St. Paul, 2,500 km west of the Australian city of Perth.

3.1. Of course, conspiracy theories emerged, which are:

UFO - According to Boston.com, Alexander Bruce in ForbiddenKnowledgeTV suggested that the plane was hijacked by extraterrestrials. As proof, he posted a video on YouTube showing a computer simulation of the plane's departure from Kuala Lumpur, in which the aircraft moves extremely fast. However, Boston.com journalist Jack Pickell also notes that the alleged UFO object in the simulation is actually Korean flight KAL672. Pickell also cites the CEO's website saying the plane's supersonic speed was the result of a glitch in the system.

Pitbull and Shakira - reportedly Pitbull and Shakira's song "Get It Started" had premiered before the flight MH-370 disappeared. The lyrics most frequently cited by supporters of this conspiracy theory are "for now it's off to Malaysia" and "Two Passports, Three Cities, Two Countries, One Day" which are related to the disaster.

The downing theory - Rush Limbaugh, according to CNN, was the first to suggest the theory of downing of the Malaysian plane, which goes like this: "The plane flies along the air corridor and all its electronics breaks down (why???) but the engines still work," the captain says. "We have to go home, we have to go back to Kuala Lumpur, we cannot fly without electronics. It's a dark night. They fly over hostile countries and are not able to let others identify them, there is no light on board, not even position lights. There was a complete failure of the electronics. Maybe some enemy country sent fighters and shot it down, then discovered its mistake and no one wants to admit what happened?"

Meteorite impact - a meteor could hit a plane. It is theoretically possible, but critics say it's unlikely. Personally, I think the probability of the event is low (but higher than zero).

Black Hole Theory - Perhaps a black hole formed over the Indian Ocean and engulfed the plane.

Numerological theories - It is about the numerological connection of the numbers 3 and 7. One of the founders of the theory writes: "Flight 370 disappeared having traveled 3/7 of the way, which was 3700 kilometers. The plane was flying at 37,000 feet when it was last seen with the use of a flight tracking software. Luigi Maraldi, 37, was one of the people whose passport was stolen. Malaysia Airlines is one of the largest airlines in Asia, carrying nearly 37,000 passengers a day. Today we are starting the 37th month from the Fukushima tragedy, which is at the 37th degree, and in which there were 37 injuries initially caused."

North Korean involvement - Other researchers suggest the plane was hijacked by North Koreans and flew to Pyongyang. Some supporters of this hypothesis argue that the plane had enough fuel to fly without being within range of a cell phone. This was proposed to explain the observation that some passenger phones were still functional after the plane disappeared.

Phantom Telephone Theory - As mentioned above, some people have proposed the hypothesis that passengers are still alive but cannot respond with their cell phones - a phenomenon known as "phantom telephone theory." This was based on early reports that family members of Flight 370 passengers checked that their cell phones were ringing after the plane disappeared, but this theory was disproved by Jeff Kagan, a wireless telephony analyst. In an interview with NBC News, Kagan said that even a completely damaged phone can still be ringing while the network searches for a connection.

Conspiracy theories about the search - Some say the governments of the United States, Malaysia, and an indeterminate number of other countries know where the plane is and are trying to hide its true location. The theory also argues that the reason these agencies didn't inform the public of the plane site is because they fear a scandal.

Microsoft Flight Simulator Theory - Photos of the interior of Zaharie Ahmad Shah's house, the first pilot, show a simulator in which he tries to land on the runway, surrounded by water. This theory says it could be a water landing simulation.

So far, we have more question marks than answers. One thing is absolutely certain - this catastrophe is extremely mysterious. It might have been a skyjacking - but what for? Seemingly the pilots had made a west or southwest turn over the Gulf of Thailand and parachuted over mainland Malaysia, running the plane wild on its way southwest - towards the middle of the Indian Ocean. But why?

As they say, the more you get into it, the more complicated it becomes. For now, we are doomed to guesswork, because the weather in the area where the remains of the plane were found is very bad, and their search has been interrupted. The second problem is the depth of the ocean at this place, which is 5000 m, and some say it is even 7000 m! And this means that extracting black boxes will be extremely difficult, if not impossible...

So we await more news and I hope that...

Robert Leśniakiewicz

Chapter 4

Boeing 777 vs. V-7?

Watching on TV and following the case of the missing flight MH370 on the Internet, I get more and more the impression that the Malaysian government either knows more than it says or wants to declare the case closed as soon as possible. I don't like that they want to consider the passengers dead so early and stop their search. Why? Is the truth about the last hours of the flight MH370 inconvenient for someone? And this is by no means the carrier, but somebody much higher up in this country?

The last signal from the plane was sent from the point described with the coordinates S44°57'29" - E090°13'43", which is a place located approx. 2500 km (another version - 2260 km) from Perth, Australia. Now, however, the distance was reduced by several hundred kilometers as the plane flew faster than expected and consumed more fuel, and therefore covered a shorter distance than calculated - the search was moved to 1,850 km west of Perth.

Of course, there is a conspiracy theory that there were stealth technology specialists on board, but was that just about them? The second conspiracy theory says that there were several tons of gold on the plane, on which - as you can see - someone had its eye... The third one tells about the family problems of the first pilot who committed suicide in this spectacular way. However, most researchers don't believe it at all.

I won't write about further conspiracy theories, because it is obvious that they are like mushrooms after rain or swords at Grunwald - numerous. Interestingly, no Boeing remains have been found so far, contrary to loud announcements - why? After all, they would have had to exist if the plane hit the water and crashed against its mirror. Well, there is a possibility that it was otherwise. The plane was flying slowly at low altitude, and when it ran out of fuel, it just landed in the water like Airbus A320-214, side number N-106US, flight UA-1549 from New York to Seattle, which made an emergency landing in the Hudson River, on January 15, 2009. That plane floated in the water and the passengers had time to leave it. But it was almost in the center of a big city, and the Malaysian Boeing landed in the ocean and apparently sank almost immediately, like the Boeing 747 Jumbo Jet from "Airport '77" movie directed by Jerry Jameson. But in the film, the plane fell in the shelf and was extracted from a shallow depth. In the case of the Malaysian machine, it went to the bottom and was crushed by the water pressure at a depth of 5000 m. This also explains the lack of remnants on the surface. They were trapped in the crushed wreck... In that case, you should look at the bottom of the ocean, not on its surface. It will be a complex and costly operation reminiscent of the search and extraction of the fourth hydrogen bomb in Palomares, Spain. The only problem is that this bomb was recovered from a depth of about 890 m - here we are dealing with a depth of up to five kilometers!

I will focus on yet another piece of information that the media has brought to light. It turns out that from 1948 until today, a total of 84 planes have disappeared in the airspace of our planet without a trace. And these disappearances took place not only in the Bermuda Triangle or the Dragon's Triangle, also called the Devil's Sea, but also in other regions of the world. Perhaps solving this one puzzle will lead to an explanation of the others?

And finally, the question: if the plane was flying in the S-SW direction, where actually? A straight extension of its flight route leads to the Kerguelen Islands (S 49°20'- E 070°20') and then to the Heard and Mac Donald Islands (S 53°06'- E 073°30'). Then there is only the icy wastes of East Antarctica ... Perhaps the hijacker/hijackers wanted to reach the Kerguelens, but they ran out of fuel? But what for? There is only the French subpolar station Port-aux-Français there, and no decent airport to land at ... What if the plane was to go even further? In that case, only the eastern edge of Queen Maud Land in Antarctica remains. Perhaps this is where the key to solving this puzzle lies? For let's not forget that this is where the Nazi V-7 flying saucers were supposed to departure from, and where allegedly were located the secret Nazi bases, in which the soldiers stay after the lost war...

Robert Leśniakiewicz

Chapter 5

Is the emergency exit in Poland?

Motto: "Curven" in German - means a CURVE political and ufological! Is it just a coincidence or a hint of time of important events...?"

Since March 8, 2014, all the media around the world have been talking and writing about the missing Malaysian plane. Of course, there is different, contradictory information and in fact, still no one knows anything! Total "holy stink" in all ways. They talk about skyjacking, transporting gold, bacteriological weapons, etc. And as always, it's all about something else ...

Analyzing the plane disappearance, I realized that it is related to my prophetic dream from two years ago! In the dream context, the matter of the missing plane is of marginal importance - as an episode and a hint of time. Of course, this is of great importance to the families of the missing passengers and to politics, ufology and all kinds of media!

What are dreams and visions?

Visions and dreams are multi-dimensional symbols, so they must be confirmed in all ways. The events of the future are hidden in inconspicuous symbols as in a pill. So they are guidelines that make you think and act, therefore I have to write about it. This is an instance of how I analyze my dreams and visions in the context of our reality, an example of which is the above-mentioned dream described at this link.[10]

The dream, as usual, consisted of several parts, and one of them concerned two passenger planes, but I had no idea what it was about because they landed in some forest road! The dream seemed important to me and was related to Robert Leśniakiewicz, which is why I described it quite accurately and published it on Facebook, and then Robert posted it on his blog. Almost two years have passed and I forgot about this

---

[10] https://www.facebook.com/notes/zofia-piepi%C3%B3rka/wyj%C5%9Bcie-awaryjne-jest-w-polsce/432513073478336

unusual dream. Suddenly, the Malaysian plane disappeared and all the media are "sounding off" about it, but I didn't understand yet that it was about the plane I saw in my dream!

Looking back in perspective of the past two years, none of us could have foreseen what these planes were about and when and where it would happen! It could have happened in Poland, but just as well in any place on Earth! Who predicted that it would happen and that it would be relevant to a completely different matter in Poland?

Meanwhile, everyone is asking the question - what is the reason for the disappearance of the most modern Boeing 777 airliner flying from Kuala Lumpur to Beijing? There were 239 people on board - including 12 of the plane's crew. The plane suddenly disappeared from the radars even though it kept sending signals automatically for some time. Reading some of the articles about the lost plane, as an ufologist and visionary, I noticed that until now only UFOs had the properties of disappearing from radars, i.e. invisibility.

So far, the mysterious disappearances of ships and planes have been recorded mainly in the famous "Bermuda Triangle". Many books and articles have been written and several films have been made on this subject.

I'm interested in technical novelties, so I paid attention to publications on the Internet regarding the patenting of "invisibility" in the USA. This means a great technical progress that has a future in the latest UFO-like technologies, e.g. invisible airplanes - about which people have been writing for years in various magazines and on websites.

Meanwhile, in "Monitor Polski" we read: "Note that this warning is correlated with the hijacking of the Malaysian plane on which there were Chinese and Malaysian experts from Freescale Semiconductors. Jim Stone believes that this is one of the actions heralding World War III. The Zionists know that Putin will not step down and that China will sooner or later get involved in the conflict. The Chinese experts on board have knowledge of secret weapons, including aircraft masking devices."[11]

Analyzing the matter of the missing plane in this context, a conclusion arises that the disappearance of the most modern passenger plane may be a test of the latest technology and the plane has landed somewhere, but no one will admit it, because of course it is the greatest SECRET, and the media will give misleading information!

Let me remind you that already during WWII the secret of German scientists and Hitler's secret weapon were the prototypes of flying saucers and experiments with invisibility - typical for UFOs. Where did they have these technologies from?

---

[11] http://www.monitor-polski.pl/cheney-impuls-elektromagnetyczny-zakonczy-cywilizacje/

Experiments with "invisibility" were conducted, among others in the port of Gdynia in Poland and possibly in other places on Earth. After WWII, experiments with invisibility were also carried out by the Americans and Russians - of course in great secret, but always something leaked to the public.

For example - in 1943 the famous "Philadelphia Experiment" with the US Navy ship took place, the case was classified for decades and "nobody knows anything" - just like in the case of the missing plane. Then the warship "moved through time and space", that is, it ended up in a different place, and some of the crew found themselves in different places, but in most cases they died or didn't regain their identity.

And now what power is conducting such tests in the Indian Ocean?! You can guess...

At this point, let me remind you what the famous "Philadelphia Experiment" was about![12]

"The Philadelphia Experiment - the name of a secret scientific experiment allegedly conducted by the United States Navy.

The experiment was to be carried out on October 28, 1943 on the American ship USS Eldridge, stationed at the US Naval Force Base in the port of Philadelphia, and ended in a tragedy."[13]

---

[12] http://pl.wikipedia.org/wiki/Eksperyment_Filadelfia

"This experiment was designed to make the powerful US navy ship invisible. They wanted to use electromagnetic generators for this purpose. The ship was in the dock and a strong magnetic field was created around it by means of direct and alternating currents. The results were amazing. Unfortunately for the crew it was a tragic experience. First, there was a hazy green light similar to the greenish fog that survivors from the Bermuda Triangle talk about. Soon it filled the entire ship, and the vessel and crew began to dissolve into thin air. Only the draft line was visible. At the same time, the destroyer appeared and disappeared in Norfolk, Virginia. This could be the result of the course of the experiment and could be related to a time shift effect. A former crew member reported that the sea trial was successful. A field of invisibility in the shape of a rotating ellipse of one hundred meters was obtained on each side of the ship. When the field power was increased, people on board began to disappear."[14]

Next...

"There are several versions of what happened during the "Philadelphia Experiment".

---

[13] http://www.tomeky.republika.pl/filadelfia.html

[14] http://www.sadistic.pl/tajemnica-zielonej-poswiaty-eksperyment-filadelfia-vt149534.html

One of them says that when the coils were turned on and the electromagnetic field was activated, a loud electrostatic "hum" appeared in the air and the entire ship was covered with "green fog". This fact will help explain what happened next, because such a fog can be regarded as a simple ionization of normal atmospheric air in a strong magnetic field. (Locations of ALIEN SPACE BASES - the author's note).

For such a phenomenon also occurs in America, in the Midwest. During a tornado or a strong storm, a specific green color of the ionized atmosphere appears.

During this experiment, when the green fog lifted, the ship was not only invisible to US operators, but also to the naked eye. One version of events mentions only the visible contours of the hull.

In turn, in another version, the ship disappeared and showed up several hundred kilometers away in a cloud of "green fog" just in front of the British aircraft carrier, the captain of which noted this fact in the logbook. It was reportedly seen at Norfolk Naval Force Base (about 375 miles north). Civilians and American soldiers who were then on the pier saw a ship appearing out of nowhere."

If the latest technologies didn't cause such a large plane to go missing, then there is another possibility...

In the Indian Ocean there is an equivalent of the "Bermuda Triangle", which is "Devil's Triangle". This means that there is a possible impact of underwater UFO Space Bases on ships and airplanes - as described by Robert Leśniakiewicz in his article![15]

This is also confirmed by "Super Express"[16]:

"Just before the machine disappeared from the radars, an unidentified spherical object flew by! (...) Researchers of unexplained phenomena from the Forbidden Knowledge portal found radar photos of air traffic over Malaysia at the time of the disappearance of the Boeing. The photos show a spherical object which the system cannot identify. It takes the shape of an airplane and ...disappears. Then the Malaysia Airlines machine also disappears... (...) The signals were sent for 4 more hours after disappearing from the radars! Where is the missing Boeing? Someone hid it on Earth or rather ...in space?!"

IvIartyn Pe writes: "Each Boeing 777 without exception is equipped with an emergency transmitter (sender/locator) for calling for help in the event of an accident on land or at sea, which automatically gets activated in the event of sudden contact with water or land. Signals from such post-disaster device are tracked by satellites. It is mandatory for all aircraft

---

[15] http://wszechocean.blogspot.com/2014/03/co-sie-stao-z-lotem-mh370-2.html?spref=fb

[16] http://www.se.pl/wydarzenia/swiat/zaginiony-boeing-777-to-ufo-porwao-samolot_386078.html

performing international flights. You can see that it didn't work either. Everything in this plane broke down?"

Looking at the photo, I thought - I've seen it somewhere...

The case of the missing plane interested and moved me mainly due to the inconspicuous photo a photomontage with a Malaysian plane in the bush of Brazil.[17]

Looking at the photo posted on Facebook, I thought - I've already seen it somewhere... After a while, on the radio I heard the news that in June 2014 the US President - B. Obama will fly to Poland and Ukraine. These two events in that order - the photo and message on radio - made me suddenly remember where and when I saw a similar picture! I saw it 2 years ago in a dream - which I described and shared on Facebook (link at the beginning of the text). On the same day, Robert Leśniakiewicz published the second article on the missing plane on his blog, where he quoted mine and his opinion on the photo posted on Facebook[18].

Quote: "...the disappearance of the most modern passenger plane may be a hijacking by a UFO, as well as testing the latest technology... This is reminiscent of the famous "Philadelphia

---

[17]https://www.facebook.com/photo.php?fbid=481082208681948&set=a.2278
00907343414.48977.227797157343789&type=1&theater

[18] http://wszechocean.blogspot.com/2014/03/co-sie-stao-z-lotem-mh370-2.html?spref=fb

Experiment" about which Robert once wrote... Similar experiments were carried out by the Nazis in the port of Gdynia during WWII..."

He next wrote significant sentences about this photo:

The photo mentioned by Eleonora is a vulgar photomontage, anyway, the plane with such fuel supply wouldn't have been able to cross the entire Pacific and land in the Brazilian jungle. Similarly, flying the other way would have had to cross the entire Indian Ocean, the African continent and the Atlantic...

Well... I got a bit nervous about this last statement so I called Robert to explain what I meant by sharing this photo (as a visionary) and to make him take it into account when writing his comments on this! I just look at reality through my visions and dreams and seek confirmations and evidence - often through associations!

Our conversation ended with Robert's proposal: "Write something about it and I will publish it on the blog."

"Fine, but I have to think about how to write it," I replied.

I started to write, but I wasn't able to do this because thoughts and various facts were swirling and I had to remit it. It turned out that in this way fulfilled part of my dream vision, which I didn't fully understand, because it was expressed in the symbol...

"1) The picture changes

I'm with Robert in some room... We stand in front of each other talking, he looks thoughtfully at the floor, and after a while he turns and disappears. After a moment he shows up with a hunting (??) or rather military weapon and gives it to me, saying:

"Here you are... shoot!"

"But I can't!"

"Take it, and shoot!"

I take the gun and look at it for a long moment, then focus, aim up at the wall and pull the trigger! I see a bullet flying out of the gun and going through the wall, then the second, third... and more, I don't know how many walls, but I think 7-8 - like a series of shots, and there was only one! I hear the echo overlap after each pass through the walls... and it worries me, because maybe someone will get hit and killed? In a dream I see it flying through the walls of houses where different people live. Robert stands and watches like me..."

I knew I had to write something and this is the weapon Robert gave me. At the time, I didn't know what the article was about and thought it regarded an article I wrote two years ago about the damaged ozonosphere! Of course, the room in the dream is Robert's Blog: "UFOs and People of the World Ocean" as well as my Facebook profile, and the "weapon" is the article that I will write. When I finish and publish it, maybe it will "hit" someone and "kill"? I'm already "scared"! This is how this part of the vision and our reality was realized in the symbol!

Meanwhile, Robert, thinking about our conversation, wrote the 3rd part on the lost plane, but with an emphasis on the scene, i.e. the Indian Ocean and the Australian coast.

Meanwhile...

"3) The picture has changed:

We stand in the forest (Robert Leśniakiewicz and I) and talk, looking ahead at the distant road... Suddenly a passenger plane appears and lands on a sandy road, slowly disappearing from our view. Somewhere on the side I hear the words: Oh fuck, Obama... I look at the plane, not understanding anything."

And in fact I didn't understand anything until now, so I unconsciously shortened what I saw regarding airplanes. It turns out to be of great importance for further events, and therefore I have to describe and analyze the same passage once more.

In a dream, we stand in a pine forest which means that we are in Poland. I looked west and against the backdrop of tall pine trees, I saw a large passenger plane flying low from south to north. It looked as if it had crash-landed on a forest road and disappeared from my sight somewhere in the forest. Looking at it in a dream, I thought: Why does such a large passenger plane land on a forest road? Maybe it's a military plane and that's why it lands at a secret military airfield?

The plane disappeared, and the image of the forest and the sandy forest road was still before my eyes. After some time, another plane appears, but I thought it was the same, so it was a repeat of what I had seen before! I see the plane slowly descending to the lane of the road. I can see a series of windows above the ground as if I were looking closely. At the same time, it seems to me to be smaller than the previous one! Analyzing this dream then, I thought that maybe I had to remember this image well and that's why I saw it twice, therefore I originally described it as one plane, although I saw two! At the same time, looking at the second plane, I hear the words reaching me somewhere from the back: "Oh fuck, Obama... I look at the plane, and then at Robert..." In my dream, I thought Robert was saying it, but the words were clearly coming from behind me, not from the side. Of course, I thought that President Obama would fly to Poland on this plane, but it doesn't necessarily have to be this way. This could mean that the second plane will disappear during this time - and so will the Malaysian plane!

When I was dreaming about those planes, President Obama was finishing his first term in office and preparing for another election. Who could have predicted that he would win the elections and come to Poland? But for what and when? We now know that the arrival of President Obama to Poland is of strategic political importance due to the situation in Ukraine and Russia. That's why in my dream I saw a military training ground with rocket cars and tanks, and in reality these are NATO troops that are already stationed along the eastern border of Poland! This is happening before our eyes and everything is confirmed, so I analyzed the dream again with particular attention to the part of the dream regarding the airplanes.

In the dream, there were two passenger planes - a larger and a smaller one, which disappeared into the forest. Has any passenger plane disappeared in Poland recently? NO! At that time, it was announced on the TVP that President Obama would arrive in June, and the media are still "sounding off" about the mysterious disappearance of the most modern passenger plane - the Boeing 777. Is it a coincidence? So in my dream it is the Malaysian plane and it is a clue and a harbinger of further events described in the symbol. But in the dream there is the second smaller airliner that lands and disappears in the same place, and it will probably happen while President Obama is in Poland.

In my dream I look at Robert, who is a retired military man and ufologist! For me, it has a symbolic meaning and is an important piece of information - a hint for the entire context, because this case is related to the military and ufology, so is the lost plane!

The question: does the colloquial and "fleshy" word appearing in the dream have any meaning: "Oh fuck (in Polish:

O kurwa)"? When I started to wonder what it meant, I was suddenly overwhelmed with drowsiness and I had to lie down, and when I woke up, the first thought that formed in my head was - "kurve" in German means a TURN, curve, bend!

I checked - in English - curve; Latin - curva; Italian - curva = in all of them it means the same - a curve...! But why in German? Does it have political significance? Is this an indication of a possible outbreak of World War III?! A terrible war, because nuclear and final? When "Mother Russia" and "Big Brother" don't get along, our socks will be "knocked off" without moving! Well, "curve" everything is clear!

In Polish, "curva" means something completely different and we all know what! So it is a blunt definition and indication of the place and time of important political events for Poland, but not only...!

"Curve" means a BEND! But political or ufological!

I realized that this common saying is a symbolic mental shortcut to indicate and properly understand the meaning of sleep in the political and every other sense. So we have a BEND awaiting us and we will either disappear like the Malaysian plane or we will rise to the occasion and understand what needs to be done. What occasion?? This is what 5th part of my prophetic dream is about! "I'm going upstairs..."

My dream foreshadows events in the near future - in a symbol, of course - as important clues of time and place and my role in it. It also means that everything I've done so far is important and matters. Who doesn't know what I have been doing and writing for years, of course will not understand what the dream portends in the symbol, no matter how I explain it!

ARECIBO... What is it?

I was wondering about the meaning of the 5th part of the sleep, as well as of an enigmatic pole above. As in the case of the meaning of the word "kurve" the answer came when I woke up and it was: ARECIBO... And what is this?

All astrophysicists know what it is! The largest radio telescope in the world is there! But it is of special importance for Poland, therefore the "pole" is an indication of the time and place in the dream and in reality. This applies to ZONE 3c 123 - "Map"[19]

I'm not a scientist and I don't speak the language of physicists or astronomers, but the indication of the high mast - the pole and the whole context of this part of the dream is understandable to me, because there is the largest Space Base... underground! There were extraordinary things happening there for a reason, which is why I have been researching it since 1992 as a visionary and ufologist. There is no coincidence here,

[19] https://www.facebook.com/notes/zofia-piepi%C3%B3rka/mapa-zasi%C4%99g-strefy-3c-123-czyli-aktywny-system-obronny-ziemi-poszukiwany-czakram/504036236288920

just like planes in a dream and the arrival of President Obama in June to Poland.

"This is what we are looking for... this is what we are looking for..."

"I woke up, and the dream images were still circling in my mind. WHAT DOES IT MEAN?! After a few minutes I started to gradually understand the meaning of the dream (...) This dream boded what would happen next. I reached for my cell phone and sent a text message to Robert. For what? I realized that the EMERGENCY EXIT is in Poland, so I had to write about it and say ... My dreams and visions precede events, although Robert doesn't believe it."

"What we are looking for ..." is important in the event of the threat of World War III and the role and participation of Poland in the conflict between Ukraine and Russia.

This dream from 2012 is confirmed by another dream that I had more than 2 months ago (February 2014) and which concerned the same place, and what is important in this dream, I also saw, among others, two passenger planes circling low in the clouds - one flew from south to north (like the Malaysian plane) and the other vice versa. The planes were circling over some place ... So this is a clue of time and place - of what? Of a secret Space Base in the ground or in the ocean? We also have it in Poland!

Describing my dream, in my conclusions I mentioned the article about the state of the ozonosphere entitled "Our blue planet ..." which I published at that time. I wrote there, among others about the need to change technology and drives. The article was published in several psychotronic groups and on Robert Leśniakiewicz's Blog, and it echoed strongly in petrified silence or ignorance ... Did they not understand what I'm writing and talking about? They don't understand now either?[20]

It has been 14 years since my lectures on this subject in 2000. As you can see at that time, scientists and the military haven't idled, working on technologies of the future, including at the Secret Base in Area 51 in the US and in the desert of the North West Cape, Australia...! ("Secret base in Australia and the program - 'Wars with aliens?' www.paranormalne.pl It's about Australia and UFOs.) The change of technology and drives will take place in a short time or not at all... because WW III will break out.

Are the existence of the Secret Base in North West Cape in Australia and the search for a lost plane off the coast of Australia or the coasts of Korea, Vietnam or China related according to journalists, ufologists, psychotronics and the

---

[20] https://www.facebook.com/notes/zofia-piepi%C3%B3rka/nasza-b%C5%82%C4%99kitna-planeta-czyli-eksperyment-jakiego-jeszcze-nigdy-nie-by%C5%82o/428863977176579

average person? Maybe some experiments with invisibility have been conducted there, and something went wrong and the plane was "moved" to another place and landed on a sandy road somewhere in the forest - as in my vision or in the "vulgar" photomontage? But no one will admit it, so some journalists come up with various theories and "holy stinks" to distract attention from this place and matter.

And now ...

"4) The picture changes

In my dream, I see a room in which there are probably 5 men. Robert stands among them, and they, intrigued, ask him questions:

"Now tell me how did you do it?"

Robert bends backwards with his gun raised and says:

"She just fired and showed ..."

The men gathered in a circle, talking in a friendly atmosphere."

Is this a group of ufologists or military officers "chatting" with Robert amicably? Good luck, BOYS! Robert teaches me to "shoot" so that it hits the right people at the right place, "for the glory of the motherland"!

- "This is what we are looking for... this is what we are looking for...!"

5) The picture changes

I go across the forest to a town or a village... I'm followed by a few people - "partisans", but then they go in different directions. I am walking up a large hill and three people follow me. On the way I pass single houses along the street like in the countryside. A man overtakes me, running to the top of the mountain, and climbs a high mast, looking around. My cousin and several other people sit on a bench under the mast. We look for something, and this is under our feet in the ground... Someone shows a strange talisman on a string... a symbolic foot and says:

"This is what we are looking for... this is what we are looking for...!"

For two years now, a group of people has been gathering around me, interested in the matter that I have been writing and talking about for years. They follow me, but none of them do anything, so they eventually leave. In a dream I walk briskly with a stick or a cane. Of course, I omitted this detail, but it's important due to the passing years. The stick in my visions and dreams is a constant element and means "traveling stick" on the way up... I have to reach the top by myself, empty-handed and with the stick, like a wanderer or a lonely explorer! In my dream, I'm followed by only three people, not a crowd! They understand what we are looking for! We are looking for traces of an intelligent HUMAN civilization from the past - about which I wrote many times taking into account my own research on megaliths! We go through the city and the countryside... Only one of them understand what to do, so he runs upstairs and quickly climbs to the top of the mast, looking around and doing something else. I was wondering what he was doing there and why?

ARECIBO!

When I was thinking about the meaning of the enigmatic pole, I suddenly fell asleep, and then came an equally mysterious explanation: Arecibo...

As you know, in Arecibo there is the largest 305 m radio telescope in the world! On the pole, they installed a device for receiving signals that focuses the waves reflected on the antenna. Could there be a second "Arecibo" in Poland?

Only then do I see that my cousin and several other people sit on the bench under the mast. I must explain that in different dreams and visions my cousin is the symbol (!) DMW. There is also another woman - a fat blonde woman who holds a strange foot-shaped talisman and waves it like a pendulum saying: "This is what we are looking for... this is what we are looking for..." Who is this woman and who does she represent? I know who this character is. It is not a woman and has nothing to do with radiesthesia. There are also other unknown people that I look at for a long time. The man sitting on the pole finally descends and sits down on the edge of the bench.

In the dream and in reality, I looked at the seated figures for a long time - thinking who they are and what they do under that pole? If my cousin symbolically represents DMW, then each character represents a different group of people from the world of science and the military. This group of people seems to be led by the fat blonde. Finally I understood. This is the research team of our "Arecibo" and that's why I eventually sit on the bench next to the "blonde". And this is the purpose and meaning of my work and life - "Arecibo"!

Do we need someone to accompany us? No! Unless a woman in a black dress comes... No no! Let some priest come here - a symbolic woman or "widow sitting like a queen on the throne" described in the prophecy of the Apocalypse, to ordain the biggest "Arecibo"? And do they have any right? There, after all, "trees burned" as in the biblical account! For me, this place is the most important astronomical, physical, technical and mystical clue, but for this hypocritical Church there is no place here! For them here is an "unpure place", because the "holy fathers" have already made such a "kurve" in this religion that no pious "lamb" will ever understand it! The same is what scientists do when they talk about their theories and Church dogmas! For them, what is white is always black...

I'm a believer, I understand what the prophecy of the Apocalypse says of this Church in the symbols. I know their various "kurven" - bends over the centuries, but it is the 21st century, we fly by airplanes and I cannot bear this hypocrisy and falsehood anymore! The prophecy of the Apocalypse in the chapters 18-20 says that this Church will cease to exist and the truth will triumph!

And Arecibo? If the "widows" could build their wonderful basilica here dedicated to the "beautiful mother of God", money would be found immediately! A lot of money! Crowds of people would work here for free. For monuments of all "saints" and churches there is always money as well, because the most important thing is "pure" faith and intention, or their next "bend" as in the Middle Ages! The time has come to "straighten" their "kurve" - "bend" with the help of politics and ufology. I hope that, sitting "on the bench" in good company, I will see this time.

The question is - how much time - years will pass until this part of the dream is realized?!

I know that in a dream and in reality this "handful of people" understand that the world and the cosmos are much more fantastic than school limited knowledge. To put it mildly and politely - in the face of the abundance of materials and artifacts, we should "jump over our own shadow" and admit that there is something wrong with the current scientific theory of the early history of mankind. They - in the vision - realized that science is wrong because it "sweeps" thousands of clues under the rug and doesn't intend to accept them! And this is the greatest scientific "kurve" - that is, the "bend" of modern science. This is a "big mistake" - a lie leading to nowhere, or rather to the very near end of civilization. And in this situation, how to explain to deceived people and nations why invisibility experiments are conducted if it is inconsistent with the prevailing false science and faith? Nobody will confess to it voluntarily! So like in the song by Młynarski - "let's do our job"!

Finishing writing this text, I heard a message on the RMF FM radio about the missing plane.

And that is the punch line of my prophetic dream! The Chinese authorities said they had picked up some signal in the Indian Ocean area, but were unable to locate it precisely. They think it may be the Malaysian plane.

I remembered the article that Robert Leśniakiewicz published a few months ago - "Is there anyone else here apart from us?"[21] and then basing on this information, I wrote the article entitled "RADIO SIGNALS from Earth, or how I sent a signal to the radio source 3C 123 in 2004!"[22]

---

[21] http://wszechocean.blogspot.com/2013/11/ktos-jest-tu-poza-nami.html?spref=fb

[22] https://www.facebook.com/notes/zofia-piepi%C3%B3rka/sygna%C5%82y-radiowe-z-ziemi-czyli-jak-wys%C5%82a%C5%82am-sygna%C5%82-do-radio%C5%BA%C3%B3d%C5%82a-3c-123-w-2004-r/751118054914069 and on Robert Leśniakiewicz's blog

"I read an intriguing article on Robert Leśniakiewicz's Blog "Is there anyone else here apart from us?" - published on November 5, 2013, where we read: "How NASA monitors signals sent from the inside of the Earth! Radio signals are sent from the deep layers of the Earth and are picked up by satellites around the world. Having broken out to the surface of the Earth, these signals travel further into space. The satellites catch and transmit them to NASA."

So maybe the Chinese accidentally caught one of such signals from FOREIGN SPACE BASES in the waters of the Indian Ocean, where there is the famous "Devil's Triangle" and therefore cannot locate it precisely?

"For the first time, scientists picked up these signals on October 30, 2013, using properly equipped satellites. Since then, the signals have been sent at intervals - our source claims. It says that these emissions have the form of a mathematical code, which makes scientists even more convinced that they are associated with a colony of creatures whose intelligence surpasses ours. Our NASA source claims that decoding these messages was not a major problem for scientists (...)

http://wszechocean.blogspot.com/search?updated-min=2013-01-01T00:00:00%2B01:00&updated-max=2014-01-01T00:00:00%2B01:00&max-results=50

Our source said that scientists are frustrated by the fact that they cannot accurately trace where these signals are sent from, and where this underground civilization is located, and they lack the technology to respond to these signals.

"Whoever they are, they know more about us than we do about them." They found a way to communicate with us, but we don't know how to answer them. (...)

Our NASA source also said it was one of the greatest and most memorable discoveries in our century.

"For a long time we thought that the universe is the most distant frontier. We have now realized that there is an unexplored area within our planet that may prove even more important to our future." (Charles George, November 2, 2013).

And this is the answer to the question regarding the last part of my dream vision. We look for something, and this is under our feet in the ground... "This is what we are looking for... this is what we are looking for..." Therefore, there will be people from Poland, and maybe from abroad, who, already knowing the precisely located and described place in Poland, will receive and send signals to this Space Base, just as I sent the signals and received the answer in the mathematical system, i.e. according to the Fibonacci formula. For this you don't need special technologies and we can answer them easily. We have our "Arecibo"... underground in Poland, not in Malaysia or in the Indian Ocean.

Everything that is important happens most often in silence and without being noticed, and other, less important matters are aggressively publicized and pass like the seasons...

In the East they are preparing a war for us... Will there be a "kurve" again - a bend like in 1939 or 1981?

And what is it about? I will explain...

During WWII, the best scientists from all over Europe worked for Hitler and his sick plans. In 1981, after the end of "martial law", many of our best scientists left Poland for the West or the South and stayed there, working for other nations. Among them was Dr. Eng. Jan Pająk - physicist, electronics engineer and ufologist. What did he do for Poland? At the end of the 70s of the last century, he published in the "Przegląd Techniczny" a project of the Magnocraft, i.e. a flying saucer, which was revolutionary and brilliant for those times in Poland. Many people reading his series of articles in "PT" considered him crazy! Quote: "he is crazy, UFOs in Poland?" But none of them knew that German scientists had done the same before and during WWII. After the war, these technologies and scientists were mainly taken over by the Americans and Russians, which are now the technical power in the world.

There was "martial law" in Poland then and there was no money or support for the implementation of his amazing technological idea, which is a pity, because today our future would look different. There would be jobs for millions of people! But then the brilliant explorer saw no future for himself here, packed his suitcase and left for Malaysia... but I don't know where exactly he is now. He wrote that due to his work as a lecturer at local universities, he moved to other islands. There, while working scientifically, already as a professor he finished his work, i.e. he made a prototype of a flying saucer. It was probably 10 years ago and, if I remember correctly, was recorded by a Malaysian television. In the reportage, Prof. Pająk explained why he did this, and then boarded the flying saucer of his own design, made of tubes, as in the description of the Magnocraft's technology diagram. He started the engine and after a few seconds it began to rise vertically upwards... and it happened on his private property, not in a laboratory! Then our TVP showed this footage on Teleexpress and Wiadomości! I was sitting in front of the TV, stunned, because he proved that it could be done, but it is a pity that not in Poland. If he is a Malaysian citizen, who does he work for? Maybe in the near future we will buy his flying saucers "made in Malaysia", and for serious money?! And what do our great physicists and mathematicians do?

I will add that before dr. Pająk left our "beloved homeland", he had given his study of the Magnocraft's technology to all technical universities in Poland, libraries of larger cities, as well as sent it to many ufologists - I also received it. Currently, his study has been available free of charge on his website for several years. Just google - Prof. Jan Pająk! Did he make a fortune from this? What is certain is that others who think about the future will benefit from it, but not Poles. When it was necessary to work on it on an industrial scale, suddenly there was a revolution and "martial law", or the great "kurve" - a BEND. And what is going to happen in Poland and in the world now? Think fast... Do you have any conclusions and ideas? Well... At that time, we were watched over by "Mother Russia", who seized all technologies of this type, because "it was not for the Poles!" And now we have "Big Brother" and still no gains regarding it? Well... "guys", so maybe our own "Arecibo"? Professor Pająk will not help us, he achieved success and has no need to come back here. And I still wander alone with the "traveling stick" like a beggar. In my dream, I still walk briskly up the hill to the "summit", and there in my vision I see that in the near future there will be a research and development team. I hope it will happen this year.

In this way, we kind of returned to the site of the lost Malaysian plane, secret technologies and experiments...

So I "shoot" - maybe it will "hit" someone and get where it should, and then there will be a radio telescope...

"God, save me from false friends, and with the enemies I will deal myself... God... protect us..."

Gdynia - April 7, 2014

5.1. My 2 cents

A small comment should be made on this material, namely: as a rationalist, I don't believe in the accuracy of the information given to us by dreams and visions. Simply because they reflect reality in our psyche, and they are probably also the result of the creative processing of signals sent to us by Aliens, one or the other. Our brains are no longer or yet adapted to their reception, hence the illegibility of visions and transmission errors that we perceive in different states of consciousness.

The missing flight MH370 is a mystery, but more criminal than ufological, although some high-ranking military and secret service officials claim that the plane was accompanied by other unknown objects. What's more, during a conversation with one of them on the air of one of the commercial broadcasters it was stated that the US government knows about the existence of UFOs and has huge archives devoted to this issue. He didn't reinvent the wheel - everyone has known it since the final Blue Book report was published. There is an interesting hypothesis about experts in "stealth" or even "super stealth" technology. Theoretically, invisibility could be obtained with the use of a cyclotron or other vacuum accelerator of charged particles, which, under the influence of powerful magnetic fields, would reach relativistic speeds and their huge masses would generate a gravitational field changing the metric of space. The problem is that enormous amounts of energy must be used to achieve relativistic speeds. And the greater the speed and the mass of the particles, the more energy must be used to accelerate them. This is obvious, and results from the Theory of Relativity and the famous formula E=mc2. Was anything like this tried during the Second World War?

Perhaps, and with different effects. As a result, however, work on this issue was abandoned. And for a simple reason - which I already described in my article on the Philadelphia Experiment[23].

Besides, it was explained much better in the 1950 by Stanisław Lem in his novel Astronauts, to which I refer Readers. The invisible plane or ship created in this way would be invisible, but... it would also not be able to see, unless it extended its sensors beyond the range of the invisibility zone, thus becoming visible. It's a physical certainty. But... something like that is already possible. The problem is only in a huge amount of energy and... the remaining consequences of the general and special theory of relativity.

And one more observation, which concerns work on antigravity. What if, instead of protons, we would accelerate antiprotons? What if antimatter was accelerated instead of

---

[23] http://wszechocean.blogspot.com/2012/03/kosmiczna-prawda-o-eksperymencie.html

matter? Would there be formed a gravitational field in the direction opposite to the vertical? Perhaps the Germans worked on it. Where? Well, in Ludwikowice. There are many indications that the famous "fly trap" is a ruin of such a device that could throw Nazi space vehicles into space. Fantastic? Of course, because antimatter has a different electric charge, and in contact with matter, there is annihilation and release of γ radiation quanta - according to the equation for electron and anti-electron: e- + e+ => 2γ. The mass of antiparticles is not (fortunately) anti-mass, although it is not entirely certain ...

On the subject of Ludwikowice and the entire Riese complex, maybe the Germans wanted to develop on an industrial scale production of ... antimatter? This would mean that in addition to the A-heads, they could also have D-heads (from the word "disintegration"?). The SF literature has made us believe that the annihilation of matter and antimatter manifests itself in terrible bursts and flashes of light. I'm afraid that this image is fundamentally untrue, and that the explosion of the D-head would only result in a powerful flash of γ-rays invisible to us, which would sterilize the land around the attack site, with a radius of many hundreds of kilometers. And that would be a real Wunderwaffe! Fortunately, that didn't happen. The problem is that it is difficult to maintain antiparticles in terrestrial conditions without an annihilation reaction.

The political predictions are also obvious. President Putin wants the restitution of Russia as a superpower within the pre-1991 Soviet Union, and as I know life, no one will stop him. The West has its own interests, which it will conduct with Russia regardless of the clamor of politics like Kaczyński, Tusk and Sikorski, and who will lose, as usual it will Poland. It is already losing, what could be expected. Eleonora is absolutely right - we found ourselves on a "kurve" at which we can easily wipe out.

Returning to the Malaysian plane - the signals from the black boxes have allegedly been found. This is what the media reported yesterday and today. If so, it means that the plane lies at the bottom of the ocean, at a depth of five kilometers, and it will rather be impossible (for now) to extract it in its entirety. So we have to wait again for this fact to be confirmed. I hope there will be...

Zofia Piepiórka "Eleonora"

Chapter 6

After 40 days...

40 days have passed since the mysterious disappearance of the cruise airplane from Kuala Lumpur to Beijing. So far, there is no trace of the Boeing 777, flight MH370, which went missing on March 8, 2014. Many traces were checked, many remains were searched for - all to no avail. Boeing 777 literally dissolved in the waters of the Indian Ocean ...

Contrary to previous views, I'm able to agree with the opinion of the former head of the Military Information Services - Gen. Marek Dukaczewski - a competent person, who in his radio speeches stated that the plane could have been hijacked either by some terrorists or by its own crew. Of course, UFOs also appeared in the background, but as a competing hypothesis rather than an obvious fact.

Today, the media reported that the plane - or what's left of it - will be searched for by a device called an underwater drone, whose task is to catch the weakest radio signals from the transmitters of the plane's black boxes, which were emitting signals three days ago, that is April 12. From that day on, no more signals were picked up, despite intensive monitoring from ships, battleships and planes. The problem is that the black boxes should have stopped working on April 7, because the batteries of these devices allow for such operating time. So either the batteries gave energy to the radio transmitters of the black boxes, or ... someone else was transmitting these signals ...

So DSV Bluefin-21 will be lowered from the deck of the Australian battleship HMAS Ocean Shield, which monitors in the area of the exposed radio signals. In addition, a large oil spot on the surface of the Indian Ocean, which may have originated from this aircraft, was also detected. This was to take place west of the city of Perth. Conspiracy theories claim that the plane was skyjacked to the American base on Diego Garcia Island - the CIA took over all the "super stealth" technology specialists and imprisoned the rest of the passengers. By the way, I'm very curious what happened to the 2.5 tonnes of gold that were also reportedly on the board of this Boeing?

Because I'm of the opinion that it could have been like this: when the plane reached a point 100 km away from the coast of Vietnam, the pilot and copilot directed it west/southwest towards the coasts of Malaysia, turning off the radio and transponder. They kept flying the plane at an altitude below 1500 m, and when they found themselves over Malaysia, they dropped the entire load to the ground and parachuted, having previously programmed the autopilot to fly the plane at an altitude of <200 m in the south-west direction - towards the least frequented waters of the Indian Ocean, where it would be impossible to find it quickly. The conspirators, meanwhile, packed the goods on the prepared vehicles and were seen no more. Could it be like that? It could! And we have the beautiful conspiracy theory!

In the next post - after Christmas, I will try to convey to the Readers other hypotheses. So...

Robert Leśniakiewicz

Chapter 7

The plane crash over Überlingen

The topic of the mysterious air accident of the Malaysian Boeing-777, flight MH-370 continues to make headlines around the world. For a change, I propose an article by Dr. Vadim Ilin on another catastrophe that took place a few years ago and also were related to many extraordinary events. I think that in this case we were dealing with something similar to the tragedy in Smolensk and Asia...

On July 16, 1923 in Chodynskie Pole, the Junkers-13 plane caught on the telegraph cables during its forced landing and fell to the ground. Military aviator Alexei Pankratiev died, and a mechanic and three students from the Air Fleet Academy were injured.

In the evening of November 17, 2013, the plane Boeing-737 flying from Moscow crashed during landing at Kazan airport. The passengers and crew died - 50 people in all. Pain and sympathy were expressed to all the families of the accident victims. In connection with this tragedy, we decided to remind our Readers of the disaster that took place over 11 years ago in the night sky over Lake Constance. There, above all, a strange, almost mystical confluence of many events took place. The consequences of this tragedy are no less dramatic.

7.1. The children flew on another plane

On the night of 1/2 July 2002, in the sky above the German town of Überlingen - N47°46'42"-E09°10'26", which is located on the northern shore of Lake Constance, there was the collision of the Russian Tu-154 (Bashkirian Airlines, side number RA-84816, flight number 2937 from Moscow to

Barcelona) and Boeing-757-23APF of the transport company DHL (side number A9C DHL, flight number 611 from Bergamo to Brussels). 71 people died, including 52 children going from Bashkiria on holiday in Spain, and their adult carers.

This tragedy was preceded by a series of unexpected events and strange circumstances. And so, thanks to a mistake made by employees of the company organizing the children's vacation, the plane on which the children from Bashkiria should have flown to Barcelona, departured without them. The company corrected its mistake within two days by organizing a special charter flight for these children.

The collision took place in the airspace under the control of the Swiss company Skyguide from Zurich, which at first didn't intend to take responsibility for the disaster. Only representatives of the German and Swiss governments expressed their official condolences to the families of the accident victims. Skyguide management only did so after two years!

7.2. Why the collision happened

An investigation into the causes of the crash revealed a series of events that occurred as a result of the carelessness of Skyguide employees. The direct blame for the crash bears the dispatcher Peter Nielsen, who controlled the airspace in which these planes collided.

On the critical night, one of the Flight Control Center's radars was not working, and there was only Nielsen on the night shift instead of three dispatchers on duty. In fact, there was a second controller in the beginning, but he, with Nielsen's approval, invited his female friend on a "tour" of the Center. This reckless behavior of both dispatchers is explained by the fact that the intensity of air traffic at that time was quite low.

As if that was not enough, they disconnected the external telephone line, only the backup line was working. But it was also unavailable - because it was used by the controller's friend talking to her friends after exploring the Center. That is why the controllers from the German center, seeing the possibility of a dangerous situation on their radars, were not able to warn their colleagues in Zurich.

To make matters worse, it was at this point that the "unplanned" plane landing at Friedrichshafen Airport appeared in Skyguide airspace, and it was this machine that needed to be dealt with immediately and first.

And on top of all this, Peter Nielsen's mistake - his decision made at a critical moment. Busy guiding the "additional" plane, he didn't hear the Boeing pilots shouting about their descent. And by mistake he gave the Russian plane an order to reduce the flight altitude.

The ground collision warning systems of both aircraft were operating normally. In this situation, the Russian copilot followed the automatics' instructions and started climbing. However, the regulations in force required approval for this maneuver from the air traffic control tower.

As a result, both planes found themselves on a perpendicular course, the Boeing vertical stabilizer cut into the center of the Tu-154 fuselage and both aircraft fell to the ground.

7.3. Admission of guilt

The media blamed Peter Nielsen for the disaster. After the crash, he had a severe nervous breakdown, quit his job, and suffered spiritual trauma for the rest of his life.

Nielsen wrote a statement in which he expressed his regret that on the critical night he became guilty of the tragedy and asked forgiveness from the family of the Bashkir victims of the disaster. Unfortunately, Skyguide management didn't make this announcement. It was only published in the German magazine "Focus", and the Russians didn't know anything about it. And that became yet another bad circumstance for subsequent events.

Nielsen felt responsible for the deaths of 71 people, and living with this awareness was unbearable for him. One can imagine the remorse and spiritual torments he suffered. And a year and a half after this terrible tragedy, a man with non-European features entered his house ...

7.4. Family tragedy

In the crashed Tu-154 there was the family of 46-year-old Vitaly Kaloyev from North Ossetia. This high-class architect signed a contract with a Spanish architectural and construction company in 1999 and left for Barcelona. His wife Svetlana and their two children stayed at home, and it was then that he was supposed to meet them at Barcelona airport to spend a vacation together in Spain.

And again a random event. When Svetlana came to Moscow with her 10-year-old son and 4-year-old daughter, it turned out that there were no tickets left for the plane to Barcelona. She was offered a flight on the Bashkir Airlines charter plane with children going on vacation. And of course, she happily agreed ...

Upon learning of the catastrophe, Vitaly went immediately to Zurich, and then to Überlingen. His daughter's body was found three kilometers from the crash site, and his son's massacred body was lying on the asphalt near the bus stop.

The incident caused Vitaly a deep depression. He returned to his homeland, where he buried the bodies of his wife and children. He was seen on their graves even at night.

In November 2003, Skyguide offered him compensation of CHF 60,000 for his wife and CHF 50,000 for each of the children (converted from USD).

7.5. Trying to be forgiven

All this drove Kaloyev desperate. He demanded a meeting with Allan Rosser - the boss of Skyguide and Peter Nielsen, and in front of cameras, he demanded they apologize to all the families of the accident victims and plead guilty to the deaths of these children. But he was denied this. Admittedly, he met with Rosser, but the man couldn't find words that would be any consolation for the man who had lost his entire family.

Kaloyev repeatedly asked the management of Skyguide to allow him to talk with Nielsen. He wanted to meet face to face with the man who was responsible for the death of his loved ones. But most of all, he wanted to hear from him words of apology and a public confession. All his requests, however, were turned down.

So he decided to go to Überlingen as a private person. It was in February 2004, one and a half years after the disaster.

7.6. Lynch

Kaloyev found Nielsen's address in the telephone book. [...] Then he went to him and showed him pictures of his wife and children.

"Look at them," he said.

What happened next, Kaloyev didn't remember. One thing is for sure that he dealt many blows with the knife he always had with him, and ran away. 36-year-old Nielsen's wife were at home with their children when she heard him scream. She ran out of her room and saw her husband lying on the floor, and the man running away. Peter Nielsen died in front of her before the ambulance arrived.

7.7. Aftermath of revenge

Finding Kaloyev was not difficult - he was in the nearest hotel. The police arrested him and drove him to a psychiatric clinic, and an investigating judge concluded that it was a crime of passion. After the trial, he was sentenced - 8 years in prison, but in 2007 a Swiss appeals court reduced his sentence - Vitaly was released from prison and returned to the country.

Public opinion in Russia, and above all in North Ossetia, was on the side of Vitaly Kaloyev. Many people believe that his actions brought the guilty to justice. While still in prison, Vitaly himself said that it hadn't relieved him - after all, his wife and children won't be resurrected thanks to this. And all the time he said he didn't remember killing Nielsen.

After returning to his homeland, he was offered to become the minister of architecture and construction in North Ossetia.

And the Swiss court found 4 Skyguide employees guilty of manslaughtering many people. Three of them were placed under police supervision and one paid a fine.

7.8. My 2 cents

Looking at everything that Mr. Ilin wrote about, I wonder if we are dealing with something similar in the case of the missing flight MH-370 - with a complete disregard of the duties by the ground staff of radar stations, which should have sounded the alarm right after the transponder was turned off on board the Boeing 777. The description of the reflection disappeared on the screen, but the echo of the plane itself was visible! So it was possible to follow its course and height. And it is said to have been done. But why after finding out that the transponder was turned off, there was no attempt to find out what was happening to the plane that changed course and flew west instead of north? After all, this alone should trigger an alarm and notify the air defense troops, because the story from the unfortunate day of September 11, 2001 could have repeated itself!

MH-370 flew over the Kra Intermarium over the Thai-Malayan border and flew towards the Indian Ocean, most likely avoiding Sumatra from the north. How did it happen that this ghost plane didn't interest any air defense militaries in these three countries? And yet they should have. What's more, they should have ordered people on duty to see what was going on - and this wasn't done. Why??? Neither Malaysians, nor Thais, nor Indonesians did it! This is completely incomprehensible - unless someone really wanted this plane to go unrecognized, God only knows where.

These are just a few questions that keep bothering me about this strange case. Recently, Discovery Channel aired the document called "Flight 370: The Missing Links" in which it is explicitly stated that the catastrophe (?) was caused by glaring gaps in flight guidance and control procedures. Just like in the case of the flight 2937. But we will only be sure when we find the wreckage of the Malaysian Boeing - unfortunately we are still far from it ...[24]

Vadim Ilin

---

[24] „Tajny XX wieka" no. 51/2013, p. 8-9

Chapter 8

How about a skyjacking?

It seems that the case of the mysterious disappearance of the Malaysian Boeing 777 is starting to slowly fade away, or is gradually muted. It is understandable because the results of the search are zero so far, no remains of the machine have been found, and - as today's "Teleexpress" reported - the location of the wreckage of the plane, which had allegedly been seen in the Bay of Bengal, or some 5000 km from the search basin, wasn't confirmed.

Australians withdraw from surface searches, which have so far been fruitless, confining themselves to underwater searches. "Gazeta Krakowska" of 29 April 2014 states that:

They will search for the plane under water

CANBERRA "The search for the remains of the Malaysian plane has entered a new stage," announced Australian Prime Minister Tony Abbott. It will cover a larger area of the Indian Ocean, as the remains are unlikely to be on the surface after such a long time. It was decided that the search would concentrate underwater using specialized equipment.

Hope is the underwater drone, which the media reported earlier on April 15, 2014.

The media continues to spread the fantastic theories and assumptions that the plane was hijacked by the CIA to the Diego Garcia base due to the presence of stealth technology specialists on board the Boeing 777.

"Wirtualna Polska" adds that:

An initial report on missing Boeing will be released tomorrow

"A preliminary report on the missing Malaysia Airlines Boeing will be released tomorrow," was announced today by the Acting Minister of Transport of Malaysia Hishammuddin Hussein.

As he added, the report will be similar to the one sent to the International Civil Aviation Organization. Hishammuddin Hussein will go to Australia next week, where he will talk about plans to continue searching for the missing plane.

Malaysia Airlines Boeing, with 239 people on board, disappeared from radar on its way from Kuala Lumpur to Beijing on March 8. So far, no traces or remains of the machine have been found. (WP.pl)

However, I'm interested in one fact - how can we be sure that the plane was landing in that sector of the Indian Ocean? Or was it, as Albert Rosales said, that the plane was hijacked, flew not southwest, but northwest, and landed safely in one of the "states" ...? It is interesting that THIS possibility is not taken into account by anyone. Why? Could the plane fly unnoticed by anyone over the territory of several countries and land, for example, in Pakistan, Uzbekistan or Kazakhstan? Pakistan is particularly suspect - it is a country with claims to India, al-Qaeda bases on its territory, and belonging to the "nuclear club". If we could add planes invisible to radars and humans, to our nuclear weapons, then ...

I hope it didn't happen, though it would be foolish not to take it into account.

Robert Leśniakiewicz

Chapter 9

The mysterious cargo?

The case has its continuation and there are another facts that raise reasonable suspicions. As it turns out, the missing plane, flight number MH-370, had 2.3 tons of mysterious cargo on board.

May 3, 2014, 6:18 pm BST / 7:18 pm CEST

- Under mysterious circumstances, a mysterious cargo was loaded aboard the Malaysia Airlines Boeing 777 night before taking off for the fatal flight. The load was not mentioned in any customs manifest. The aircraft was to carry 4,566 kg of mangosteen - an exotic fruit used in cancer therapy, as well as a load of lithium batteries, which were part of a separate shipment. The batteries weighed 200 kg, but the shipment they were in weighed 2453 kg. So what was the remaining 2253 kg of cargo?

These questions were raised when Malaysia Airlines announced the closure of the assistance centers in Beijing and Kuala Lumpur for families of 239 passengers of Boeing 777-200ER.

These centers were closed after rescuers ceased a fruitless search for the missing jet, that focused on the distant waters of the Indian Ocean off the west coast of Australia.

The mystery started with a statement for a Malaysian newspaper, by a spokesman for a company supplying batteries, in which he said that he wouldn't reveal what the remaining 2,253 kg load had been.

"I can't reveal anything else due to the ongoing investigation," the spokesman told a reporter for The Star newspaper today. "Our legal advisor told us not to tell anyone anything."

The spokesman said he couldn't even name the battery manufacturer because the information was confidential.

When asked why the mysterious cargo was not mentioned in the manifesto, Malaysia Airlines replied to the newspaper that the rest were "radio accessories and chargers."

The airline's statement says the unspecified cargo was "declared as radio accessory", despite it wasn't even mentioned in the manifest that was released to the public last Thursday.

A group of 11 terrorists who had ties to al-Qaeda were questioned to find out whether they had anything to do with the disappearance of the Malaysia Airlines plane.

Suspects were arrested in the capital city of Kuala Lumpur and in the state of Kedah last week. They were members of a new terrorist group that was about to carry out bomb attacks in Muslim countries.

The hearings were the result of an international investigation involving the FBI and MI6, and regarded terrorists between the ages of 22 and 55, including students, people having strange professions, a young widow, and young businessmen who were all thoroughly questioned about flight MH370.

Almost 2 months after a plane bound for Beijing went missing shortly after taking off from Kuala Lumpur airport, no trace of it was found, despite a large-scale search costing millions of pounds.

The plane is believed to have fallen into the ocean with 239 people on board. An officer at the Malay Security Services Counter-Terrorism Center stated that the arrests had taken place due to the high probability that the plane's disappearance was an act of terror.

At the moment, this is basically the only option. And the load not mentioned in any manifesto could have been the reason for it - even if it was "only" two tons of gold, it would still have not been a thing to despise by an "honest" terrorist! The question is, how was it done technically? Theoretically, it could be done like this: the pilots hijack the plane, turn off the communication and the transponder, and then fly over mainland Malaysia to throw the cargo and parachute ashore, where the rest of the gang with a truck waits for them. Then they collect the valuable cargo and disappear, melting somewhere in Asia with a pile of cash in hand... Meanwhile, the plane continues to fly led by the autopilot until it runs out of fuel, and plummets into the ocean. End of drama.

But that is only one possibility. What interests me most is that the plane could carry some radio apparatus (let's say) on board, which worked all the time and needed batteries for that. And it was about this apparatus. The plane could go to Kazakhstan (where Russian military bases are located) or to Uzbekistan or Diego Garcia (where American bases are located) or to Pakistan, Afghanistan and other "states" where people interested in such cargo are present. So, in this whole affair, this shipment plays a primary role. Malaysia is one of the economic "tigers" that produces various electronic toys - including interesting boys in aviation uniforms in many countries ...

By the way, I'm reminded of an incident from the 1980s, which was mentioned in the Polish press in 1983:

9.1. More about the ghost plane

London, PAP - On Thursday was canceled the search for the wreckage of the Learjet 25 plane, which, after mysteriously covering a distance of 2,500 km between Vienna and the waters around Iceland, fell into the Atlantic. The disaster may have occurred 200 miles south of the island. The machine could therefore rest on the bottom about 180 meters below the water surface, which makes it impossible to reach the wreckage.

Various hypotheses about the causes of the tragedy continue to be advanced. The plane with 3 people on board took off on a test flight to Hamburg[25], 720 km away, but for unknown reasons at an altitude of 14,000 meters flew over Germany, the Netherlands, the North Sea and Scotland, then disappeared from the radar screens. The reconnaissance planes sent didn't see any sign of life in this machine. No one was sitting in the pilot's cabin or in the passenger compartment. It is likely that after activating the automatic pilot, there was a sudden decompression with the

---

[25] All highlights by me - Robert K. Leśniakiewicz

oxygen supply cut off. Lack of oxygen causes loss of consciousness in 15 seconds, and death within 6 minutes. At this altitude, everything freezes to the bone because the temperature is -56°C.

According to the participants of the rescue operation, the captain of the machine broke the basic safety rule by leaving the cabin after turning on the automatic pilot. Even if there were noticed any traces of life on the plane under such conditions, it would have been impossible to rescue the passengers. After two times getting within 10 meters of the ghost plane, the machines accompanying it flew away and the Learjet at the speed of 17 km/min. (1020 km/h) headed towards its destiny.

Observation of the path traveled by the plane showed that in the area of 100 km north of Frankfurt am Main, the plane unexpectedly deviated from its course.

As the most likely scenario for the tragedy, the British pilots indicate a deliberate decompression in the machine as part of their experiments.

"Głos Szczeciński", May 21, 1983[26]

---

[26] In 2008, I contacted the editors of "Głos - Dziennik Pomorza" regarding this information, but I didn't find out anything new about it, and the topic wasn't discussed further. However, together with Stanisław Bednarz, we found new information on this subject on the Internet. If you are interested, please visit our book "Tajemnice

Interesting - isn't it? And how much it resembles some of the facts about the flight MH370! Of course, scientific experimentation is out of the question, because it wasn't what it was about, but it is possible that the unfortunate Boeing 777 was depressurized and the people aboard died on the spot. Another question is whether the depressurization of the airplane was due to a failure or an intentional act. If the version about the secret stolen cargo turned out to be true, such a scenario would fit the known facts. Therefore, two fundamental questions should be asked:

Could the pilots open the Boeing 777 cargo hatches and throw in any items, and ...

... could pilots (or other people, e.g. hijackers, terrorists) leave the plane by parachuting?

These questions should be answered by the designers of this type of aircraft and aviation experts. After all, there is a known case in which the hijackers left a passenger plane using parachutes. Of course, this is only a hypothesis and the truth could have been completely different ...[27]

---

katastrof lotniczych".

[27] http://www.dailymail.co.uk/news/article-2619388/What-havent-told-cargo-MH370-Mystery-deepens-missing-flight-claims-loaded-2-3tonnes-items-not-listed-manifest.html

So await more information!

Robert Leśniakiewicz

Chapter 10

The flight MH370 satellite data will be released after months of waiting

Inmarsat and Malaysian officials said they would release the raw data from the satellite. Families have been waiting for this information for months. The data will allow independent experts to analyze what happened on March 8. "Their intentions will be supported by deeds," said the husband of one of the passengers.

Kuala Lumpur, Malaysia (CNN): *After months of silence, data from the satellite on the MH370 flight will finally be made public to the families of the victims of this drama. Until now,*

Inmarsat, the company whose satellite was receiving signals from the missing plane until the last hour of flight, claimed that it was unable to publish these data. However, On Tuesday, Inmarsat and the Malaysian authorities said they would seek the disclosure of the data.

10.1. Flight MH370 data will be shared

In line with our commitment to greater transparency, all parties are working to publish the data transmission log analysis and technical description, Inmarsat and the Malaysian aviation authorities said in a joint statement.

Where is this data?

"It must also be noted here that the transmission log data is only one of many pieces of investigative information," officials said.

However, this statement doesn't say when this data will be released. But the release of this raw satellite data could allow independent analysis of what happened on March 8, when Malaysian Airlines flight MH370 disappeared with 239 people on board.

Several relatives of the plane's passengers were unsure what to do with the announcement.

"Their intentions must be supported by actions, so I will wait and see what happens," said K. S. Narendran, whose wife was on the plane. "Second, this is only one part of the data that was used to conduct the search," Mr. Narendran told CNN correspondent Don Lemon. "A larger dataset is to be made available in time."

CNN airline analyst Jeff Wise said that "the can will be opened" when the data is released.

"It will produce many theories and erase many other theories," he said.

In other words, releasing this data might give "a better idea of what happened at that time."

Inmarsat "works" to make the raw data available to the public:

"Dark" part of the Malaysian Boeing 777 flight MH370 - it is not known what happened to the plane between Perak and the place of reappearance on radar. It is only known that it flew at an altitude of 4000-5000 ft/~1330-1660 m

10.2. Conflicting Statements

On Monday (19 May), the incumbent Malaysian Communications Minister said the government asked Inmarsat to release the data. Malaysian officials told CNN reporters their government didn't have any raw data. But workers from Inmarsat said their company gave all the data to the Malaysian government "at an early stage of the search".

10.3. Reaction of the Flight MH370 passengers' families to the film

"We shared the information we had and this investigation is to decide what and when will be revealed," Inmarsat vice president Chris McLaughlin said last week. But a senior Malaysian official told CNN the government needed Inmarsat's help to pass the data on to families "in a representative manner."

"We tried to be as transparent as possible. We have no problems with disclosure of data," he said.

Whenever information comes out, it can help answer questions from critics who are skeptical about the location where officials were looking for the plane. Some scholars investigating the disappearance as well as passengers' families began to criticize the authorities for the lack of information as to why the search was focused in the eastern Indian Ocean.

Did the Inmarsat data send MH370 search and rescue teams in the wrong direction?[28]

Message from Cannes:

The filmmakers are controversial about the flight thriller MH370.

Saima Mohsin & Holly Yan (CNN)

---

[28] http://edition.cnn.com/2014/05/20/world/asia/malaysia-missing-plane/?hpt=hp_t1

Chapter 11

Does the Bermuda Triangle have anything to do with the disappearance of the Malaysian plane?

The missing flight of the MH-370 is such a mystery that reminds us of the possible existence of the Vietnamese Bermuda Triangle. But let's take it with a grain of salt. Officers from several countries, dozens of planes and ships comb the South China Sea and the Bay of Bengal after the Malaysian Airlines plane mysteriously disappeared with 239 people on board, and many suspect it may have something to do with the Bermuda Triangle.

It has become inevitable that this disappearance would bring up comparisons to the infamous waters where ships and planes vanish without a trace. A few days ago, a Malaysian politician tweeted: The new Bermuda Triangle has been detected in Vietnamese waters, where all vessels equipped with electronics sink. This outraged many people whose comments were unkind and who then apologized for them.

The term "Bermuda Triangle" was introduced in 1964, but was spread around the world ten years later when Charles Berlitz, whose family created the popular series of language courses, wrote a book about it. Berlitz believes that the legendary continent or subcontinent of Atlantis really existed and is responsible for the mysterious disasters and disappearances of ships and planes off the coast of Florida.

Over the years, many theories and hypotheses have arisen to explain this mystery. Several writers have extended Berlitz's theory of Atlantis by suggesting that the mythical city lies at the bottom of the ocean and uses its famous "crystalline energy" to melt ships and planes. Other, more exotic theories suggest there are time portals and Aliens - including stories about underwater Alien bases. Still other people believe that the explanation lies in extremely rare geological and hydrological natural phenomena.

Others suggest that the Malaysian Airlines plane disappeared over a body of water that is directly opposite the part of the globe where the Bermuda Triangle is. Isn't that an amazing coincidence?

It seems mysterious and strange when we look at a map or a globe and see that the search area is exactly on the opposite side of the world, not to the Bermuda Triangle, which is in the North Atlantic, but to the Caribbean Sea. Excluding geographical deliberations, no one knows where the plane is. Perhaps it fell and sank in the South China Sea, off the coast of Malaysia or elsewhere. In fact, rescuers suspect that the plane didn't enter the ocean at all, but may be in the jungles of Vietnam, where search and rescue teams have also been dispatched. And since the plane could make a turn after the last radar contact, the search area is huge.

11.1. Why the Bermuda Triangle?

The biggest problem that connects the mystery of flight MH-370 with the Bermuda Triangle is its disappearance, however, the Bermuda Triangle doesn't exist. It was demythologized back in the 1970s, when Lawrence David Kusche investigated the alleged strange disappearances in the Bermuda Triangle. Kusche has exhaustively researched the strange "mysterious disappearances", and Berlitz and others have written about it and created a story that is based essentially on errors, distortions and mystery - and in some cases, on fabrication of entire stories - and all this was passed down as proven facts.

In his book "Trójkąt Bermudzki - Tajemnica Rozwiązana" (Polish edition: Warsaw 1983), Kusche noted that several authors writing about the subject hadn't made any specific investigations, but most often took information from earlier authors who had done the same. In a few cases, there are no records of ships and planes lost in this triangular water cemetery - they never existed beyond the imagination of the authors. In other cases, the ships and planes were real - but Berlitz and others had neglected to say that they had "mysteriously vanished" in the nasty storms.[29]

---

[29] L. D. Kusche unfortunately carried out his own "research" in university libraries, which consisted in searching for press clippings about disasters. Besides, he chose them so that they would support only his theses. NB, I caught him on an obvious forgery about the Dragon Triangle. Mr. Kusche brazenly lowered the tonnage of the missing ships in order to downplay the matter. According to him, not fishing trawlers went missing there, but "some" cutters. Besides - according to Japanese calculations, and what Kusche says - 521 cutters and boats were lost there in 1968, 435 in 1970 and 471 in 1972! After all, this means that in 1968 alone, about 1.43 units disappeared at sea every day! - at least one a day!!! Assuming that each fishing vessel has 8-12 crew members, it means that about 5,000 people disappeared at sea without a trace! Can 5,000 disappearances be ignored by the authorities? THERE'S NO WAY SUCH THINGS ARE IGNORED!!! See http://hyboriana.blogspot.com/2014/04/trojkaty-

It should also be noted that the Bermuda Triangle is heavily frequented by cruise and merchant ships, and it is logical that more ships sink there than on, for example, the less traveled routes of the South Pacific. But the waters in the "hell triangle" don't have such a high number of mysterious disappearances.

The flight of the MH-370 and its disappearance is a real mystery, but the fact that it happened isn't that unusual, so nothing unexplained or supernatural happened there. The search area is large and remote (about 2,000 km off the coast of Australia) and sea currents can move the plane's debris far away. The fate of flight MH-370 is unknown, but an explanation could appear any day.

11.2. Latest news from Australia

On June 27, 2014, "Teleexpress" informed that Australian investigators reported that the passengers of flight MH-370 had been no longer alive after losing communication with the plane due to depressurization of the cabin, and the plane had continued to fly, being guided by the autopilot ... So it would be a carbon copy of the catastrophy of the Greek plane, flight HA-522, which crashed in Athens as a result of depressurization of the cabin - but more on that later.

11.3. My 2 cents

So everything indicates that the scenario of the hijacking and looting of the Boeing-777 cargo, carried out by either the pilots or thieves among the passengers, was most likely played out. History knows the case where a hijacker - a certain D. B. Cooper - first skyjacked the Northwest Airlines Boeing 727, flight NA-305, which flew from Washington, DC to Seattle, WA via Minneapolis, MN, Great Falls, VA, Missoula, MO, Portland, OR, and Spokane, WA, then parachuted with a ransom. Already in the air, the passenger sitting in the seat at the end of the plane handed the flight attendant a card with his demands: the airlines were to provide him with $200,000 and 4 parachutes, otherwise he would have detonated the bomb he had on his lap.

His request was granted and he received what he wished. The man in turn released all passengers and crew except the captain and the flight attendant, who became his hostage. The hijacker requested that they fly to Mexico, but this wasn't possible - the Boeing 727 couldn't make this route without refueling, so he agreed to refuel in Reno, NV. The hijacker consented, however, under two conditions: the plane must have been flying below 10,000 ft/~ 3,000 m at 200 mph/320 km/h with the back hatch open. The plane took off towards Reno, followed by 5 fighters following its flight and the Boeing back hatch. The skyjacker at one point parachuted with $200,000 and disappeared into the darkness and thicket 35 mi/56 km north of Portland, WA ... He was never caught, though the police and the FBI bent over backwards to hunt him down.[30]

Halina Krahelska, who described this case in her book "SOS" (Warsaw 1988), also states that six others people tried to do this stunt, but they didn't succeed.

They didn't - that's true, but for example pilots or other people on board the Malaysian Boeing-777 could do it. The plane descended, crossing the airspace over the Malay Peninsula, where it was freed of the golden cargo, then thieves parachuted, leaving the plane with dead passengers and crew to their fate. It could be so, because something like this is indicated by the flight parameters of the aircraft from the point of the last radio contact with the aircraft, to the last radar contact over the Strait of Malacca. It is hard to suppose that they threw out the precious cargo above the ocean and jumped into the water. They had to do it during the flight over the Malay Peninsula - where, after taking the cargo on the ground, they holed up in Malaysia or Thailand.

I will only add that it was not the work of amateurs, but professionals were working there. It was a brilliantly executed

---

[30] Recent FBI research indicates that this aerial pirate killed himself in a parachute jump - his body fell into the river and the money was scattered by a rapid stream of water ...

secret service style operation, and it was about something so valuable that the plane and the lives of more than 200 people were sacrificed without hesitation to get it. And there is no space here for UFOs and Bermuda Triangles or Squares or other similar phenomena. I believe that the investigation into this gloomy case should go in this direction ...[31]

Benjamin Radford

[31] Mother Nature Network - http://www.mnn.com/earth-matters/wilderness-resources/stories/is-there-a-bermuda-triangle-connection-to-the-missing#ixzz35ZUI8Ygj

Chapter 12

MH-17: The tragedy in Ukraine

Five months after the mysterious disappearance of the missing MH-370 flight, another Malaysian plane crash occurred. This time over Ukraine - or rather its south-eastern Donetsk Oblast, near the village of Hrabove/Torez.

On July 17, 2014, at 4:21 PM EEST/3:21 PM CEST, at the point described with the coordinates: N48°08'42"- E038°38'54", the Boeing 777-200ER, side number 9M-MRD, flying from Amsterdam-Schiphol (AMS) to Kuala Lumpur (KUL) went down. The departure took place at 12:15 pm CEST, and ETA was to be at 06:10 pm MYT. 283 passengers and 15 crew members died, mostly Dutch and Malaysian citizens ... There were many (over 100) AIDS specialists on board who flew to a science conference in Melbourne, Australia, as well as 80 children.

As it soon turned out, the plane was shot down by - so far unknown people. The 9K35 Buk/SA6 Gainful or S-300/SA10 Grumble surface-to-air missiles were probably used to shoot it down. Their operation requires high qualifications, and the people who launched the rocket had to know what target they were firing at, experts say. It has been suggested that these rockets may have been launched by Russian troops or by separatists supported by them.

I don't believe in the hypotheses getting through our heads by Polish propaganda and that of the so-called "free" world. There is an ancient Roman principle saying that it was done by someone who has some good, some benefit from it. Do the Russians or the separatists have any benefit from this? No, none. On the contrary - the world remembers the shooting down of the South Korean Boeing 747, flight KAL-007. Is President Putin stupid enough to allow himself to repeat it? No, he's not that stupid, and that's what differentiate him from our politicians by God's grace and bestowal. And let's not forget that the Ukrainians already shot down one Russian airliner in 2001 and didn't suffer any consequences for it. This is first.

Secondly, the Ukrainian authorities didn't close the airspace over the fighting sites, and they should have done it. It is clearly their fault. And all the advocate's ploys of our propaganda are of no use here - the fault lies with Kiev. Air corridors over Ukraine should have been closed! This wasn't done, and put travelers in the greatest danger. And the tragedy happened. And here is another interesting thing: the Ukrainian Security Service provided recordings of the talks of Russian separatists about shooting down Boeing 777. What does this mean? Well, this means that Ukrainian security service listened and recorded conversations of separatists also before the catastrophe. They listened and controlled, so they knew about the planned attack and ... they didn't do anything!!! They didn't warn, nor did they pass this information on to anyone who could prevent it. And another thing - there was released a footage that allegedly shows a Russian rocket launcher without one rocket. Question: why didn't the Ukrainians get it before the border with Russia? After all, this would have constituted the so-called hard evidence that the Russians had shot down the Malaysian Boeing. And this wasn't done - why?

Thirdly, a hysterical propaganda campaign against Russia begins, which, as you can see, has been in preparation for some time. It is very useful to the Americans, because the United States needs a war that will be the driving force for the American economy. That's why President Obama took the floor so quickly, and President Komorowski, of course, pointed to Russia as the cause of this tragedy. Interesting, there had been no investigation yet, and he already knew who was behind it! And yet it is enough to wonder who actually benefits from it. Russia? - certainly not. And speaking of propaganda, it reminds me of the 1980s, when the slogans were written on the walls: "TV lies", "DTV lies as it lied," etc. etc. - but now the situation has changed - the supposedly independent television has become the propaganda machine of the West. So only the direction has changed - the rest is the same.

Fourth - the whole case smells wrong and reminds me only of the arson of the Reichstag. It was a perfect excuse to sort out the left wing in Germany, and now it is a pretext to join the Ukrainian-Russian war on the side of Nazi epigones, ex-Banderites and the UPA supporters, and to extend this conflict to the whole of Europe. As a consequence, the European Union will emerge from it economically weakened, and the US will be able to introduce another Marshall Plan for it, which will be a period of prosperity for them. Therefore, it is primarily in the US interest to unleash this war.

The whole thing looks like a provocation and is as plain as a pikestaff. The goal is obvious - to convince the world that Russia is bad and should defeat Russia, imposing sanctions and starting a world war - of course to the joy of the United States, which as a result will not fall apart into 50 independent states (already 35 states show centrifugal tendencies) and will improve its economic prosperity. And this is probably what is about this media circus, into which Western propaganda transforms this tragedy.

How does this relate to the disappearance of the MH-370 flight? According to the legend, it was carrying 2 or even 4 tons of gold. In addition, there were passengers on board, including a dozen electronic engineers and IT specialists. They were said to be specialists in defense systems, espionage systems, etc. In the case of the MH-17 flight, there were AIDS specialists on board. Maybe this fact is the key to this mystery? Liquidation of specialists in areas that constitute the vital interests of all of Humanity? Of course, this is another conspiracy theory, but sooner or later it would be raised, so I only anticipated the facts.

I'm terrified and at the same time astonished by the thoughtlessness with which Polish politicians repeat their mantra about "sanctions", about "punishing Russia" ... What do they count on? The reconstruction of the Jagiellonian Poland? They don't realize that in the event of a war with Russia, which they crave so much, Poland would be exposed to its first blows, and the first bombs and rockets would be launched against it! Why? Well, because the main east-west communication routes run through Poland. In the assumptions of World War III, it is clearly stated that 40-70 nuclear warheads with a capacity of 200 kt - 2 Mt of TNT were to be fired toward Poland, which will turn our country into a radioactive desert. This is a physical certainty! I don't know what do our piteous "politicians" count on? The miracle of John Paul II? Or maybe on the protection of Poland by the mantle of the Virgin Mary? There is nothing worse than crank stupidity!

Individual phases of the nuclear war in Poland: as you can see, the goals are all major cities in our country. The nuclear strikes were to be performed by our today's allies in the case of the movements of the Soviet troops to the west. These plans are still valid with slight modifications ...

I will follow the development of the situation, but I'm afraid that I will never find out the truth from the Polish media, which are at the service of other countries and don't represent Poland's interests. I don't trust them anymore. The wheel of history has made a full turn, and history may repeat itself. Because it repeats itself as many times as we let it ...

Robert Leśniakiewicz

Chapter 13

More about the Ukrainian tragedy of MH-17

When I wrote the last material on this topic, I asked myself what other people thought about it all. I checked Onet.pl and Interia.pl forums. I rejected the slurs of rabid Russophobes, because apart from the gutter and foul words, there was nothing meaningful there. Below are only representative statements from among several thousand that are on the Internet. And most of them point to the culprits ...

I read vile comments striking the Polish raison d'etat. You don't learn any lessons from history, but just tap at the keyboards thoughtlessly in order to exist. Poverty in Poland is increasing, economic emigration is growing, unemployment and homelessness as well, but there is a lot of venom and saber-rattling on the forums. I wonder from where comes the favor of Poles towards the West, the USA and Ukrainians who never have their own statehood or identity. After World War I, over the West and the Curzon Line, Piłsudski fought for Poland's borders getting along with the Ukrainians. Before and during the Second World War, the west turned its back on us, allowing extermination of 6 million Poles by Germans, slaughter in Volhynia, and the hiding of the facts about Katyn. After World War II, they sold us to the Soviets and wanted Poland to be within the Duchy of Warsaw. In the 70-80s, the West conspired against the legal Polish authorities and the order that had been established in Yalta. After 1989, the West wrecked our entire industry, processing and agriculture. Where did so much venom to Russia come from? After all, thanks to Russia we gained independence three times in the 20th century. After the First World War from Lenin, after the Second World War from Stalin and after the Cold War started by the west, from Gorbachev. It is not Russia that is the cause of our unemployment, economic weakness or mass emigration. It is not Russia that straightens bananas and cucumbers, claims that a snail is a fish, prohibits us from building and launching ships, or order us smoke sausages, fish and cheese in a certain way. We have to look at actuality realistically.

I wouldn't call terrorist, a dozen or so thousand insurgents against the governments formed by the junta in a coup d'état. For me, they are more likely partisans. They fight in their own area where their mothers, wives and children live. They don't terrorize. They fight and defend their cities. Besides, there are people from that land, as were their ancestors. Into the government, broke people who were ethnically alien to the Slavs. Some have only recently learned the language. Tymoshenko, Jacyniuk, Klitschko, Kolomoyskyi, Poroshenko are all Michnik's countrymen. I invite the UPA supporters and Banderites to thumb down.

They got heavy weapons a month ago in Artiomovsk in the base of the Ukrainian army. Tanks, armored personnel carriers, Grads and Uragans, as well as other heavy artillery. That is why Bandera followers have been getting a terrible lashing lately. The Banderites are not mythical at all. The Right Sector named after Stjepan Bandera is not a myth, but a hideous reality, and as in the good old days, it brutally murders the defenseless, such as in Odessa.

There's nothing to explain. Only the Ukrainians were interested in the dynamics of the situation. I know the guilty ones. It is undoubtedly the Kiev junta. Besides, let's not forget about Volhynia. The number of murdered people decreases from year to year - today it was announced that it was about 100,000 - this is probably still more than in Katyn .. In 2-3 years, when the last witnesses of this genocide die, it will turn out that in Volhynia, there was a wedding picket fight. I remember the first estimate of ~ 400,000 killed Poles. Now, from the Institute of National Remembrance, I have heard about 60,000 refugees and several victims.

I can already see panic in Kiev, Washington and Brussels. What propaganda will the proponents of "freedom and democracy" create when it turns out that the Malaysian Boeing was shot down by a Bandera fighter? Why do the Polish-language media don't report the fact that the witnesses just before the explosion saw a second object approaching the Boeing and it was definitely not a rocket? The whole world is investigating the matter of this "mysterious" second object, and in Poland silence, only on the day of the incident in Panorama at 6 p.m. a journalist spilled the beans about the second object flying to the Boeing. Since then, the Polish-language media has silenced this thread. FB "Protest against the support of Ukrainian nationalism by the Polish authorities."

The question arises: why didn't the Ukrainians warn all airlines and ban all flights over the area where the war has been taking place, knowing that the insurgents had come into possession of such a long-range BUK weapon. The separatists warned not to fly over their territory, but nobody cared about it. And why, although the captain of the Boeing asked to fly at an altitude of 10.7 km, he was ordered to fly at an altitude of 10.1 km?

In 2001, the Ukrainian army mistakenly shot down a civilian plane over the Crimea with an S200 launcher. Over 70 people were killed! To this day, the Ukrainian Army has not learned to fire it! It is this weapon that was used - of course, not without great intelligence. If the USA hasn't started propaganda about the cruelty of the Russians so far, it proves that it is not them, but the wonderful Ukrainian soldiers. Why has this news not been released so far? Well, because Americans can tell nonsense so openly, because certainly not only American satellites have photos from that area.

And what for flanneling and repeating false toss of Bandera followers? After all, these revelations about hiding the boxes, about the refusal to hand over the bodies didn't hold water. Maybe the Banderites themselves were looking for the boxes to destroy them, because there may be facts that will be difficult to explain.

This case become more and more suspicious. Various facts come to light, but most often they are media facts. So there is no reason, and politicians are not allowed to pass sentences at this stage. Unfortunately, our government doesn't remember about it. I wonder how Hoffman will talk to the Russians once he comes to power after he accused Putin of murdering the plane's passengers?

Immediately after the downing of the plane, the Ukrainians knew that it was shot down with the BUK system, and earlier they hadn't allowed the plane to fly at a higher altitude! It all adds up to a planned provocation!

They turn your brains into mush. Until there's an independent investigation, Kerry can only talk to a wall.

"Rather clear" ... "We know with full confidence" ... Well, everyone in the world knows that Ukrainians never lie, so if they say that they didn't shoot down the plane, they certainly didn't ... As you can see it is already clear that the "USAs" either simply don't know who was shooting, or they know, but the shooting was the doing of the people who, from the propaganda point of view, shouldn't have done it ... They will play dumb, chirp about "trust" and heat up the temperature playing it out in propaganda against the Russians ...

These clowns manipulated by the hunchback noses are going to war with Russia, but that could backfire at everyone. The Polish nation is for peace and cannot be manipulated.

I'm a reasonable person and I don't believe a single word of the Ukrainians.

Attention!!! IDIOTS are actively operating on internet forums and they discredit normal, sober-minded Poles. IDIOTS see Russian agents everywhere. Unfortunately, stupidity cannot be cured, you can only pity them and hope that they will not reproduce. I greet the sober-minded.

Why the US didn't want to comment on Smolensk and in the case of the Malaysian plane "it points"?

A rush of Ukrainian trolls on the forum.

I will be honest. I was a moderate observer supporting Ukrainians. After what it did, Ukraine lost all my backing. In my opinion, Ukraine has gone to the worst act of terrorism. First, Ukraine gave back Crimea without a shot, shouting and looking for people willing to fight instead of using the Ukrainian regular army. The West help, the USA do something - this is Ukrainian false courage. Now Ukraine shot down the plane just to blame Russia. It was not Russia that needed a downed civil plane, but Ukraine. Ukraine turned out to be mean and without humanity.

And what for these victims, this war and the involvement of Europe, especially Poland, in the defense of the Banderites? If eastern Ukraine doesn't want to be under the rule of the Banderites, it is Poland and Poles who should help it gain independence.

I feel sorry for you, because you don't see that the case of Ukraine is the desperate agony of the USA which, seeing its poor end, at all costs seeks war??? Why don't our mass media of DISINFORMATION write anything about BRICS??? The emergence of the gigantic military-economic bloc Brazil-

Russia-India-China-South Africa, formed a few days ago in Brazil, causes the scales of power to move to the other hemisphere and the dollar-based currency system is COLLAPSING!!! Why don't any gossip rag writes that Argentina has signed huge contracts with Russia for joint oil and gas extraction in Patagonia, and the construction of a huge nuclear power plant by Russia??? Why didn't anyone mention that Putin brilliantly undercut US interests in South America, which made Wall Street and the Jewry ruling it furious??? And now the MOST IMPORTANT!!! Turkey, despite being in NATO, is the FIRST country that chose GOLD settlements !! Ankara already settles an account with Iran in this way and made an offer to Russia to switch to gold, leaving the green rag! Haven't you noticed that Turkey is strangely silent about Ukraine??? It is a slow and painful end to an era and the US will drown the whole world in blood to prevent that from happening. And now I expect epithets like a Russian agent and a smelly Russkie - all the best!

And has anyone on this forum wondered at least once if is it really Russia's doing? By strange coincidence, at the same time, Israel invades Palestine and murders civilians! And on TV journalists say only about the plane. Don't believe the TV propaganda. Start thinking, people.

And what will this guy say when it turns out that the plane was shot down by Western favorites? Banderite murderers are under special protection, and this gives much food for thought. They blame Russia with no evidence, and they seeks to set the world on fire with a terrible war.

And now a more extensive statement on Ukrainian-Polish relations:

Wake up Poland!: To the Memory of Our Nation, because we can't count on the Memory of our kosher government operating on a string of USrael ...

JULY 11 - BLOOD SUNDAY IN VOLHYNIA

As F. Budzisz writes - "in the years 1943-1944 it is difficult to find a day when the murders of the Polish population were not carried out, and these were the days when thousands were killed, for example on 10, 11, 12 July and 30 August 1943. July 1943 is the height of the crime of genocide. It was the BLOODEST SUNDAY in the history of the Polish nation. In terms of the territorial range, the number of victims and the barbarity of the perpetrators, the crimes committed that Sunday outweigh any other crimes ever committed against the Polish population in one day. Over 10,000 people were then murdered using the most brutal methods, in nearly 100 towns, villages and settlements of Volhynia." In seven churches in Volhynia, Ukrainian nationalists from the OUN-UPA killed over 1,000 believers, not sparing children receiving their First

Communion, nor priests. The vastness of the area where these crimes were committed and their timing (Sunday) proves that it was an action, carefully planned and co-ordinated by the OUN management.

Here are just a few examples:

July 11, 1943. In the vicinity of RADYVYLIV, Dubensky Uyezd, over a dozen Polish estates were burnt, and their inhabitants murdered.

July 11, 1943 JEZIORANY SZLACHECKIE, Dubensky Uyezd, Ukrainian nationalists murdered 43 people of Polish nationality.

July 11. 1943 LINIV, village, Svinyuska volost, Horokhiv county, Ukrainian nationalists murdered the entire village ...

July 11, 1943 KYSYLYN, seat of the commune, Horokhiv county. A large group of Ukrainian nationalists surrounded the Polish population gathered in the local church ... Some people left the church, 62 people were murdered then. The rest - about 200 people - went to the presbytery and took up a desperate defense on the first floor ... After midnight, the attackers withdrew ... The wounded were helped by local Ukrainians, opponents of the UPA.

July 11, 1943 RUDNYA, village, Kiselynska volost, Horokhiv county, the Polish population was attacked by Ukrainian nationalists ... the whole village was burned to the ground. About 100 people were killed.

July 11, 1943 ZAMLYCHI, village, farm, Khorivska volost, Horokhiv county ... Ukrainians murdered 118 people of Polish nationality.

July 11, 1943 GUCIN, Polish colony, Hrybovytsia volost, Vladimir-Volynsky Uyezd, a group of several hundred Ukrainian nationalists attacked the colony at dawn. The perpetrators drove about 140 people in total (35 families) into an old, unused forge, which was bolted, poured over with petrol and set on fire. Among the Dante's scenes in the burning smithy, several men managed to breach the wall and some people escaped... Most, however, died in the flames. Three of Jan Krzyszton's children were saved by an old Ukrainian woman. The next day the children were forcibly taken away and drowned alive in a well ...

July 11, 1943 KALUSOV, Polish colony, Hrybovytsia volost, Vladimir-Volynsky Uyezd. The UPA group drove all the women to the farmer Grabowski's barn, and the men to Urbaniak's barn, and murdered them all. A total of 107 people were killed ... During the slaughter ... several torturers burst into the house of Józef Fila, where they murdered his wife, 23, as well as torn a few-month-old child, pulling its legs, and placed the remains on the table.

July 11, 1943 MYKULYCHI, seat of the commune, Vladimir-Volynsky Uyezd, a unit of the UPA (about 600 people) came there on over 80 carts ... They murdered people in individual houses, or took entire families to the forest and killed them there. In this way, the entire settlement was slaughtered ...

July 11, 1943 BYSKOPYCHI, village, Mykulychi volost, Vladimir-Volynsky Uyezd, Ukrainian nationalists carried out a mass murder of people driven to the school building ...

July 11, 1943 OCTAVYN, colony, Mykulychi volost, Vladimir-Volynsky Uyezd ... a group of torturers (UPA) carried out a murder in the Octavyn church. After the massacre, it was set on fire with grenades ...

July 11, 1943 DOMINOPOL, village, Verba volost, Vladimir-Volynsky Uyezd, the UPA murdered the entire population of Dominopol, about 60 families (around 490 people) ... They killed with knives, axes, pitchforks, etc...

July 11, 1943 TERESIN, Verba volost, Vladimir-Volynsky Uyezd, Ukrainian nationalists murdered 88 adults and 28 children of Polish nationality in the Teresin colony, 116 people in total ...

July 11, 1943 KRYMNE, village, Krymne volost, Kovelsky Uyezd, Ukrainian nationalists murdered the Polish population gathered in the church for the Sunday service.

July 11, 1943 TURIVKA, colony, Korytnytsia volost, Vladimir-Volynsky Uyezd, Ukrainian nationalists murdered 49 people of the Polish population. 22 people were thrown into a well.

July 11, 1943 OZHESHYN, colony, Porytska volost, Vladimir-Volynsky Uyezd, Ukrainian nationalists murdered 306 people of Polish nationality ...

July 11, 1943 VYDRANKA, village, Korytnytsia volost, Vladimir-Volynsky Uyezd, Ukrainian nationalists murdered several dozen people of Polish nationality ...

July 11, 1943 ZYGMUNTOVKA, colony, Mykulychi volost, Vladimir-Volynsky Uyezd, Ukrainian nationalists murdered one hundred and several dozen people of Polish nationality ...

July 11, 1943 VYTOLDOVKA, colony, Porytska volost, Vladimir-Volynsky Uyezd, Ukrainian nationalists murdered several dozen people of Polish nationality.

July 11, 1943 HRENIV, village, Hrybovytsia volost, Vladimir-Volynsky Uyezd, the Ukrainian nationalists attacked the Roman Catholic church-chapel during the service. Father Jan Kotwicki was killed at the altar ... Elsewhere in Hreniv, in two barns, the torturers murdered about 200 people.

July 11, 1943 NOVYNY, village, Korytnytsia volost, Vladimir-Volynsky Uyezd ... On that day (at the hands of the UPA) 66 people of Polish nationality were killed in Novyny.

July 11, 1943 STENZHARYCHI, village, Korytnytsia volost, Vladimir-Volynsky Uyezd, a unit of the UPA commanded by "Bloody Potap" murdered 80 Poles.

July 11, 1943 SMOLOVA, village, Mykulychi volost, Vladimir-Volynsky Uyezd, Ukrainian nationalists massacred

Poles. Among the victims was the family of Jan Wargacki ... the pregnant wife had her belly cut open to "help her to give birth to the cursed Pole"... 19 people were murdered in total.

July 11, 1943 PORYTSKA, town, seat of the commune, Vladimir-Volynsky Uyezd. During the Sunday service at 11.30 am the Bandera followers attacked the Polish population gathered in the local church. They threw grenades at the church aisle, and opened fire with small arms and machine guns, causing a massacre, which made people fall to the church floor in a row. The acolytes died at the altar, and priest Bolesław Szawłowski was seriously wounded and pretended to be killed. After this initial cannonade, the Bandera followers entered the church and killed with headshots all those who were still moving ... After this massacre, the torturers brought straw and set fire to the church ... At that time, heavy rain fell and extinguished the fire ... Fr. Szawłowski died, completing the group of 500 people who died on the same day in the church or beside it ...

July 11, 1943 KORYTNYTSIA, seat of the commune, Vladimir-Volynsky Uyezd, Ukrainian nationalists murdered Fr. Karol Baran from the local parish. After stabbing him many times, they cut across the body with a saw in a wooden trough.

July 11, 1943 ZABOLOTYE, village, Hrybovytsia volost, Vladimir-Volynsky Uyezd, Ukrainian nationalists murdered 76 people.

July 11, 1943 NIKOLAYPOL, colony, Verba volost, Vladimir-Volynsky Uyezd, Ukrainian nationalists murdered 50 people ...

July 11, 1943 VOLYA SVIYCHIVSKA, colony, Verba volost, Vladimir-Volynsky Uyezd, Ukrainian nationalists murdered the Polish population ...

July 11, 1943 SVIYCHIV, settlement, Verba volost, Vladimir-Volynsky Uyezd, the Bandera followers murdered several hundred people of Polish nationality. The slaughter began with an attempt to blow up the walls of the local church, which was a sign for murdering Poles ... gathered at the Sunday service ...

July 11, 1943 STASIN, Polish colony, Hrybovytsia volost, Vladimir-Volynsky Uyezd, an armed unit of the UPA surrounded the colony, women with children as well as men were driven separately into barns, and murdered - using fanciful torture ...

July 11, 1943 ZVEZHYNETS, colony, Verba volost, Vladimir-Volynsky Uyezd, local Ukrainian nationalists murdered Łukasz and Antonina Gaczyński. Łukasz was thrown alive into a well and lapidated. Antonina was decapitated, and Ukrainian children pulled her head on the road, holding the hair.

July 11, 1943 BOZHA VOLYA, colony, Verba volost, Vladimir-Volynsky Uyezd, the Bandera followers threw Antoni

Stelmach and twelve other young boys alive into a well, and they drowned or where lapidated."

Let me remind you that it was only ONE DAY.

On the hypocrisy of the Polish government and the media:

July 11 marked the 71st anniversary of "Bloody Sunday" which initiated pogroms and genocide against Poles. What did our? Polish? media have to say about it?

First, I looked at the ones that shout that they are the most patriotic.

"Niezależna" - not a word.

"Gazeta Polska" - article "Heavenly sotnia" I thought it was about it, but it turned out to be about the heroes of the Euromaidan.

"Gazeta Polska Codziennie" - not a word.

"Nasz Dziennik" - there is an article "Let's Fulfill the Duty of Memory". Bravo for that. "Wyborcza" - there is an article "Today is the 71st anniversary of the Volhynia massacre. "It is not nationalists who dictate how Ukrainians think about Volhynia," but rather not about crimes but about modern Ukrainians who don't sympathize with the UPA.

"Wprost" - not a word.

"Newsweek" there is an article "Today is the 71st anniversary of the Volhynia massacre." Bravo.

"Polityka" - not a word.

And next:

You didn't give the surname because you meant the President of the USA. He murdered the Yugoslavs, Afghans, Iraqis, and previously the Vietnamese. Or maybe you can tell me what kind of weapons the "heroes" fight with in Syria? Are mercenaries fighting in Syria with the legitimate government, using American weapons, righteous? What do USAs look for in Ukraine? They wanted to be stationed closer to Russia, and Russia didn't allow it, and that's why you call them creeps? You are probably a Polish Catholic as insults and hatred are the basic trait of people like you. Show me the country where Russia bombs civilians. And the USA? What wrong did the Russians do to Poland nowadays? After the famous crimes, Ukrainians still praise Bandera and have territorial claims to us. You are pathetic. Note that nobody cares about our opinion anymore. Maybe bears at the Arctowski station still have some respect.

Why do American Jews tell half-truths? It is obvious that the Buk missile system comes from Russia (it was produced there), and the Banderites are equipped with it, and other inoperative one is in possession of the soldiers of the Donetsk Republic. The problem is why the Bandera followers don't confess to the downing of the plane, and blame the soldiers of the Donetsk Republic. In the world, 65% of people dying in armed conflicts are killed with weapons manufactured by concerns owned by American Jews.

Together with a local newspaper, I bought the Friday "Wyborcza". I was reading a column (probably) by Mariusz Zawadzki from Washington. And what did I see? Obama therefore imposes sanctions on Russia because all nations (including Ukrainian) have the right to self-determination, and Russia threatens the order that has prevailed in Europe since World War II. The author probably thinks we are stupid. Do Americans recognize the right of Kurds or Basques to self-determination? Especially the former are aggrieved, because it is a nation of several tens of millions, living in several countries, including NATO's Turkey - so it probably doesn't have that right. Do Palestinians have the right to self-determination when the US supports Israel? And the second point. It can be recalled that the Americans broke the post-war order by establishing the mafia statelet of Kosovo. But that's nothing. Zawadzki probably forgot that at the turn of the 1980s and 1990s (i.e. several decades after the war), there were colossal changes on the map of Europe. More than a dozen new states were created, including Ukraine, and somehow the United States didn't shout about breaking the post-war order. I'm not a Russia supporter, but this country has the same right to express its aspirations as the USA, Germany or Poland do. And the

"Wyborcza" author didn't even provide his or the editorial e-mail. That's why I answer him on this forum. All the best.

The whole world knows that separatists are eavesdropped, but not they themselves. It is absurd to think that after the disclosure of earlier recordings, the separatists continued to allow others to record them, burdening themselves and Russia. If the Ukrainian secret service intercepts this type of information so easily, the conflict should have ended long ago - they would have known every move of the separatists.

And so on and so forth. And more and more people don't believe our propaganda bullhorns. For me, the most emphatic fact of the Ukrainian "friendship" is that, despite the friendly gibberish, the Ukrainian authorities didn't revoke the embargo imposed on Polish goods. That's it. The embargo is an act of economic war which is waged against Poland. There's nothing to discuss. It's like with visas to the US - there is a lot of talk about friendship, but friendship develops through personal contacts. And these are limited by visas, so there is no question of friendship. Therefore, I would sooner believe that the plane was shot down by Ukrainians than by Russians or separatists.

Coming back to Ukraine, Ukraine has NEVER apologized to Poles for its crimes. The Germans apologized, the Russians apologized, even twice, and the Ukrainians - never! There is only one conclusion - the Ukrainians have never come to terms with their bloody past, and the spirit of Hitler and Bandera is doing well there, which we saw during the Euromaidan. That's why I don't believe the Ukrainians and those who get in their - you know where - without soap and vaseline.

Unfortunately - it is difficult to disagree with this. Personally, I am sure that it was the Ukrainians who shot down the MH-17 so that the world would declare war on Russia and plunge into a bloody brawl again.

Robert Leśniakiewicz

Chapter 14

The tragedy and farce of MH-17 with the fascists in the background

The case of the downing of the Boeing-777, flight MH-17 took an unexpectedly comical turn. Some sources say that the flight MH-370 and MH-17 relate to the same Boeing-777, with the same people on board ... You can read about it on the pages of "Wolna Polska": http://wolna-polska.pl/wiadomosci/ujawniamy-dowod-zdjeciowy-zestrzelony-samolot-mh370-cz-2014-07

What do I think about it? Leaving aside any moral aspect of this news invented and propagated by some sensationalist hyenas preying on human misfortune, which I consider extremely reprehensible, of course such an operation would have been possible, but wouldn't have it been too expensive?

Besides, what happened to the passengers on an authentic MH-17 flight? Something had to be done with them. Were they shot? Poisoned and thrown into the sea? In addition, there is another problem - the plane. Since it was the repainted Boeing-777 with the side number 9M-MRO to seem to be the plane with the side number 9M-MRD, such a hoax would have been discovered quickly, for example thanks to the numbers of the parts of which these machines were built. Some time has passed since 8 March, and on Diego Garcia, the engine numbers, chassis and other parts of the plane could have been changed. It would have cost a bit of time and effort, so the case seems to be an ordinary hoax.

I thought so until the day before yesterday.

On July 24, 2014, the Court of Human Rights in Strasbourg found Poland guilty of human rights violations against two Arab terrorists held in the CIA secret prison in Stare Kiejkuty. It was a bizarre trial in which the European Union took the side of terrorists and demanded from Poland to pay some horrendous compensation to the members of al-Qaeda, who these Arabs are de facto. Not a word was said about whose prisons these were. And namely, they were the prisons of the CIA, or the US government. It is not said who tortured the prisoners there - Poles? Not Poles - but Americans, torturers and executioners from the CIA. This wasn't said. I'm astonished and terrified by the enormity of the hypocrisy of the USA and the EU, which has made Poland, a comfortable - because guided by blind, greedy, obedient and slow fools acting against Polish national interests - a whipping boy. This is exactly the same lie as the lie about "Polish extermination camps". This is a total defeat of Polish diplomacy focused on Ukraine, in which prevail the Nazi epigones of the OUN and UPA - bandits who have on their conscience ethnic cleansing in Volhynia or in the Bieszczady Mountains, for which they have never stood trial! What is supporting the epigones of fascism if not promoting it? Is there no paragraph against this in the Polish Penal Code?

How does this relate to flights MH-370 and MH-17? As you can see, Americans and Western Europeans can afford any meanness, any dishonesty towards even their allies. The EU and NATO are helpless in the face of the conflict behind our eastern border, and in the event of an expansion to our lands, they will not take any action except barking at Russia and sending OSCE observers who, too, are unable to do anything but watch. And even if NATO sends its troops to separate the fighters, there may be purges that NATO troops will not stop in any way - the example of Srebrenica in Bosnia, where 8,000 Muslims were murdered in front of the Dutch UNPROFOR battalion is terrifying and symptomatic.

And finally, something relaxing for fans of numerology and superstitions related to it. The downing of the Boeing-777 (a triple lucky seven) took place on 17 July - two sevens more. Unfortunately - for Italians, for example, 17 is as unlucky as 13. Besides, the plane's registration number contained as many as two M letters - that is 13th letter of the Latin alphabet ... You can say the luck of these three sevens was reduced by 17 and two 13! Bad luck! It had to happen!

Robert Leśniakiewicz

Chapter 15

MH-370: The Mystery of
the Missing Flight

The submarine USS Capelin (SS-289), launched on January 20, 1943, disappeared on December 2, 1943 in the Molucki Sea area. The ship either blown up in a minefield or fell victim to a giant sea monster.

Recently (March 8, 2014) a passenger stratoliner belonging to Malaysia went missing. What if it was hijacked by an Alien pilot, shot down by a super rocket, or sank into the ocean?

Don't take this, Reader, to be pointless considerations. You already, unlike the author, first of all "know" what in "reality" happened to the Malaysian Boeing 777-200, flight MH-370. It may happen that while you are reading this text, they will show you the remains of the crashed plane on TV. Or the whole undamaged stratoliner, allegedly hijacked by terrorists, who landed in some "hospitable" country. Or ... Nevertheless, don't believe that we intended to present to you the certificates which were fixed at the time of this issue. Better do yourselves an overview of the official - "only correct" - information below. And then, as you know, you will not find our proposal more adequate than the nonsense that "competent people" feed you.

15.1. In a web of lies

Even if you - Dear Reader - was shown the "hijacked Boeing", think about it: couldn't the "three sevens" be skyjacked by a loner pilot (by the way, what the other 11 crew members were doing - were they watching? or maybe they were in collusion?) or a commando of super-pilots? Yes - they could. There are two possibilities. The pilots-hijackers were aliens for whom all technical arcana (especially Boeing's avionics) was a piece of cake - something like a children's pedal car for Schumacher. The second possibility is that they were just pawns in a wide-ranging plot - at the level no less than in the suicide aircraft attack on the Twin Towers of WTC in New York.

It's a shame to read and listen to statements issued by representatives of the authorities and competent bodies claiming otherwise. Why? Facts, not guesses, could be listed for a long time. We will cite here only one, or rather "two in one".

In a Boeing-777, a crew is practically unable to disable the ACARS transponder (AZN-W) which allows air traffic controllers to see the aircraft's marking on the radar screen and thus identify it. Of course, I assume that terrorists are also educated people and can read this article too - so I won't reveal the secrets of some technological innovations built into the ACARS device after the attack on New York.

Let me put it this way - pilots cannot turn ACARS off completely. And even if they did, it would be with all the functioning electronics on board. You have to be a dilettante believing that the rest of the crowd are also laymen, to convince people that this stratoliner was maneuvering in the air for several hours. And in addition "over the very surface of the ocean, escaping from radar range". And yet we were fed such nonsense. As well as many other lies. For example, the claim that it was "technically impossible" to trace the location of the plane passengers' cell phones, which were working for several hours since the incident began.

The web of lies, in which representatives of the authorities, investigative brigades, self-proclaimed experts wrapped the unfortunate MH-370 flight can only be explained with two circumstances. Each of them is important for all of us - both for a petrified materialist and a lover of mysteries.

15.2. Is the truth somewhere nearby?

Fact number one: If Aliens are not taken into account, the hijacking or destruction of an aircraft like the Boeing-777 can only be cynically used in the interests of some of the passengers on board. I'm talking, of course, not about "Ivan", whom it would be convenient to accuse, as soon as the version about the act of terror sounded, but about certain "initiates". Were there any on board? There were. And not few.

It should be said that on that day two dozen representatives of the Freescale Semiconductor company, dealing with the development of the latest semiconductor defense technologies, appeared on board this plane. Who else of the "keepers of secrets" went missing along with the Malaysian plane - only God knows. An interesting hypothesis is promoted by employees of Western secret services on their nonpublic Internet forums. The hypothesis goes like this: an important "initiate" or several were kidnapped before the plane took off -

which explains the fact that passengers' cell phones were working on communication networks. These passengers were "false targets" in the "cover" action to skyjack and/or destroy the plane. Of course, the huge amount of false details thrown to the media by various commentators and instances is explained above all by the disinformation operation perfectly performed by "unknown interested persons". The logic of this hypothesis is indisputable. The tactic of this type of action in the language of secret services is described as "smashing the whole caravan in order to extract one and only raisin".

The second circumstance is of greatest importance to all of us. That circumstance is the fact that all such ultra- and super-expensive tracking devices - including America's "total covering by satellite observation" have turned out to be completely powerless. Just like hundreds of specialists using them, and thousands of officers and soldiers of special services from different countries. In order to cover up this shocking circumstance, they were totally overstating some villains' abilities while underestimating the capabilities of the ACARS system.

And won't you, reader find this thought cynical? Most likely, the mystery of the MH-370 flight lies in one - but for most of us - rhetorical question. Who can guarantee that something like this won't happen again? But not the "disappearance" of the plane with passengers on board, but with the weapons of mass destruction.[32]

15.3. My 2 cents

And we finally have a sane voice in an ocean of gibberish. In fact - it looks like it was a skyjacking organized by a secret service. A secret service of a country that wanted to know the secrets of Freescale Semiconductor. This company, based in Austin, TX - according to the American Wikipedia - has branches in 19 countries and employs 17,000 people. In March 2014, 20 employees of this company went missing without a trace. The company specializes in semiconductors and structures of radio devices for cars and other vehicles - including space vehicles. Apart from that, they dealt with computers and information technology. The company created the first all-transistor duplex car radio in 1969 as well as the first prototype of a cell phone - already in 1973! Besides, it was there that were created the MC68000 processor and other parts that led to the computer revolution in 1984, and which were used in computers produced by Apple, Atari, Commodore, Sun and HP. Currently - that is, in the first decade of the 21st century, the company deals with the development and production of consumer microelectronics. So there is something to fight for ...

Could someone hijack a plane with a weapon of mass destruction on board? Of course - for this purpose, strike and subversive forces are trained. Could someone give a guarantee that this will not happen? As far as I know - no one could. There is no 100% security - because there is no such thing as perfect condition.

And one more thing. On the 17th of July, 2014, the Boeing-777-200ER, flight MH-17 from Amsterdam to Kuala Lumpur was intentionally shot down over Ukraine. 283 passengers and 15 crew members died. There were over 100 AIDS specialists on board who were flying to Melbourne, Australia to take a part in a science conference. Again, the question is: was it an accident or a deliberate provocation? Because in this context, the first question to be answered is not who shot down this plane and with what, but why exactly this one and not another??? Of course, this tragedy caused the hurricane propaganda attack on the Russians, but that wasn't really what it was about. The goal was to make someone of the specialists unable to speak in this conference. Could that person's words have been related to the spreading epidemic of EVD in West Africa - known as Ebola?

Either way, there seems to be a connection between all these events. Something has escaped someone, someone has released a demon into the world and is trying to hide it from the public by shutting people's mouths regardless of the cost and sacrifices ...

Stanisław Danilin

Chapter 16

Flight MH-370: We just need to know

Once the gifts are under the tree, it is obvious that someone has placed them there. Even if it was five years ago or more. Then the shadow approaches the tree. For us, although we don't believe in ghosts, we don't know what is in the dark.

We humans are experts at seeing patterns and meanings where there really is something more than a series of loose points. The points that we can quickly fill with a pen are called by our brain. The order in which we complete these points depends on who we are and what we have in the background. And the end result will be different for each of us.

None of us want to live in a world where there are too many difficult endings, too many points out of context, and too much uncertainty. We want our world to be understandable. Won't an excessive dose of the Unknown lead us to a headache? Our search for understanding often leads to the filling of the unknown with supernatural elements. We see in it the hand of God or the intervention of Fate. Or a conspiracy. Whichever option you choose, it suits one or the other.

Now we are dealing with the trauma of the flight MH-370 missing, which, despite the search and efforts of leading experts, has simply not been found. And so far no one understands why.

Therefore, no one is surprised that newer theories appear every now and then with some regularity. And so, a few days before Christmas, the statement of the former director of the not very famous airline company Protues Airlines - Marc Dugain was published. Dugain - unknown outside the French airline zone - stated that the plane probably entered the US zone and was shot down by the Americans.

The reason could be that hackers (from North Korea???) took control and they were flying over the US Navy base on Diego Garcia. The only way to remove the threat was to shoot down the plane. This is evidenced by the fact that the United States says it doesn't know what happened to the plane, and witnesses in the Maldives say they saw some large plane flying over them after MH-370 had gone missing.

Anyone following the MH-370 events will remember that witnesses in the Maldives never tried to find it and that it was simply a fanciful story. But our collective memory can be very short, and something untruth can easily become true when it fits the pattern.

So the search for the MH-370 is still fruitless, and there is no trace of it and no evidence to suggest the truthfulness of the Maldivian witness accounts. The plane didn't appear over that place at all, but disappeared over other place and was flying in a completely different direction.

But as long as we don't know what really happened, people all over the world will continue to draw lines between points on a piece of paper that is constantly changing its shape. All in an effort to make the unknown known and life more understandable. Because we want it so much. Although life is sometimes beyond real mysteries ...[33]

16.1. My 2 cents

---

[33] „Dagens Nyheter", December 25, 2014 -
http://blogg.dn.se/markligheter/2014/12/25/nar-vi-bara-maste-fa-veta/

Clas Svahn wrote these words on December 25, 2014, and on December 28, at 07:24 WITA / 23:24 GMT on December 27, the Airbus 320-200 plane marked PK-AXC went missing off the coast of Indonesia. The aircraft was owned by the Malaysian[34] airline Air Asia. Its flight number was QZ-8501 and it was flying with 162 people on board from Subarai (SUB) to Singapore (SIN) - ETA at 08:30 SGT. And I wonder, wasn't that a signal ahead of this catastrophe?

It is strange that bad luck had it in for Far Eastern machines: on March 8 this year, Boeing-777, flight MH-370 mysteriously disappeared somewhere over the Indian Ocean.

Another Boeing-777 of the same company, flight MH-017 was shot down over Ukraine on 17 July this year and no one can convince me that the seven is happy!

---

[34] The PK-AXC is an Airbus A320-216 in Y180 configuration delivered to AirAsia Indonesia on October 15, 2008. PK is INDONESIAN registration. AirAsia Indonesia is an INDONESIAN airline (owned by the international AirAsia group with headquarters in Kuala Lumpur, but ONLY headquarters). The machine made a flight designated as QZ8501. QZ is the flight designation of the INDONESIAN airline AirAsia Indonesia. AirAsia Berhad MALAYSIAN flights are marked with the AK code. MALAYSIAN machines have registrations starting with the country code 9M. But, as you can see, talking and writing about the MALAYSIAN plane sells better ...

Well, and now this Airbus from Indonesia. And nearby is the Strait of Malacca, where strange things happen, like in the Bermuda or Dragon Triangle ...

But were they just random disasters? In the first case, one can safely say about the skyjacking. In the second one, it was clearly the downing by the Ukrainians. I wonder what caused this tragedy? Terrorists again? - because certainly not Little Green People, which will probably soon be announced by "ufologists" and the fans of the conspiracy theory of history ...

Clas Svahn

Chapter 17

The conspiracy of the secret services of Israel?

Two more Malaysia-related airplane crashes give food for thought. Because was the Malaysian Boeing 777, flight MH-017 accidentally shot down over Eastern Ukraine on 17th of July 2014, despite that several other planes flew there? This is what I find strange that the Ukrainians shot down this and no other plane. I will omit here all the nonsense told by the supporters of the conspiracy theory of history as well as the urban legends they create that were quickly put into circulation, and I will focus only on one but significant fact: Malaysia is the only country whose parliament has recognized Israel as a terrorist state.

I asked my friends and here's what they told me:

E.K.: Read this post of my friend on FB: Marek, don't fly over Indonesia on a Malaysian plane. There, the Americans fire energy weapons. Surely JJ knows something :-). Another Malaysian plane was destroyed (in cooperation with a small nuclear country :-)). It's obvious why. Because the Malaysian Parliament is the only one in the world (!) which recognized Israel as a terrorist state ... (The author is a civil aviation pilot)

M.R.F.: There are no coincidences, even in a hot case like this. I don't believe that some fate has dominated this line. I'm inclined to the fact that someone hellishly want to intimidate passengers of all airlines. Perhaps this is a terrorist act, or perhaps a doing of one of the states that tests new ways of annihilation. Maybe the danger doesn't come from the surface of this planet, but from one of the artificial satellites as part of Star Wars, which is underway and now entering a new stage. (The author is a retired military airman)

Foxbat: I don't think MOSSAD would have any political or strategic interest in downing the Malaysian plane. Events suggest that flight MH-370 had rudder problems and other big problems - loss of radio communication, loss of transponder, etc. There may have been a fire in the tail section of the aircraft. Any plane with such problems would have to return to base.

Flight MH-370 couldn't, because its rudders didn't work. By my mind, it fell somewhere into the ocean between the Maldives and Sumatra. Its remains, therefore, were searched in vain in the wrong place in the South Indian Ocean. I'm not sure if the Malaysian government considers Israel a terrorist state. But the fact is, we don't have any diplomatic relations with it. Malaysians are not allowed to visit Israel, and vice versa, no Israeli is allowed to enter Malaysia. We treat them as terrorists. And the worst ones! (The author is a retired Malaysian military aviator)

Aga Draco: I guess it's a coincidence. The first of these three has not actually been found and is still a mystery. The second one was shot down, and the latter may have been affected by unfavorable weather conditions or some sudden incident on board, to which the crew didn't have time to react, but we still have to wait because the search continues.

What wonders me is a fate (?) hanging over the Malaysian airlines.

In addition, this year there were other disasters in various countries that are not so memorable because they weren't so characteristic.

Smok Zorzakowy: I'm reminded of the warning of the alleged contactee who supposedly learned to build electromagnetic and communication systems using the six-dimensional structures of space. He was given not only the construction diagrams of such devices, but also a warning against nuclear tests, which cause severe disturbances not only in our four dimensions. In addition, mirror craters of disturbance reportedly form on the other side of the Earth and can cause air crashes. The problem is that Malaysia's antipodes are Peru, so this hypothesis remains among loose speculations.

I would be more suspicious of electronic weapons testing or disturbances due to the proximity of the secret area. In the end, weather conditions, suicide bombings and equipment flaws. It is also possible that there are terrorist extortions. Recently, Sony has become the target, so it's worth considering if it's something on this scale.

And yet! They all suspect either Americans or Israelis, or both ... Coincidence?

Unfortunately, only the bodies and remains of the Indonesian Airbus wreck, flight QZ-8501, which fell into the Java Sea, are currently being extracted. I hope that examining its remains will give an answer to the question of what caused this crash and perhaps also answer questions about the last flight of the Boeing 777, flight MH-370, because I'm sure that the two cases are related. For if it turns out that this was a sabotage, the implications of this act could be significant and unpleasant for Israel. The killing of several hundred people in three plane crashes might have had a specific goal: to undermine the position of the Malaysian carrier that has so far enjoyed an excellent reputation. This might have been a prestigious and, above all, economic retaliatory strike against Malaysia. And it already is, because the shares of Malaysian carriers have fallen by a few percentage points, which translates into a loss of millions of dollars ... Either way, it's very bad.

There may also be other considerations that we don't know about yet. Perhaps some space weapons are tested over Indonesia, Malaysia and other Southeast Asian countries - similar to the thastra described in the Mahabharata - which causes loss of consciousness and confusion for air and space pilots ... Australia is nearby with the United States Air Force and Space Force bases as well as the United States Navy base on Diego Garcia. On such "toys", uniformed boys have always worked and will keep working.

Anyway - the matter begins to clear up: instead of Aliens and/or holes in Space and Time, we may have a ruthless fight for world domination. And if anyone has any doubts, please read the Old Testament with understanding, and pay attention to what ethnic and religious purges, what extermination of entire tribes and nations, what crimes against humanity were committed in the name and with the name of Jahve on the lips! After something like that, murdering a few hundred people is really a small piece of cake. Or such a case of Jedwabny - a flagship example of pressure exerted on Polish governments.

Jedwabny's lie shows exactly the mechanisms of operation of Israel's services in Poland. Well, but that had a specific goal: to extort from Poland $60 billion in compensation for Jewish property lost during World War II. Interesting: The Jews were murdered by the Germans, Ukrainians from the UPA, Russians from RONA, Šauliai and many more, but Poles are to pay for it? And that for what reason? How long will this paranoia go on? Poland was invaded from two sides, occupied for 5 years, then it was forced to undergo an unacceptable regime because of the vile betrayal by the Western Allies, and is Poland to be punished for it?

And in the context of these three catastrophes, it is worth considering whether the crash of our government Tu-154M machine, side number 101, which happened in Smolensk on April 10, 2010, wasn't also caused by such a subtle sabotage? The pilots were flying the plane as they have should, but there was a bomb on board (let's say a device) that damaged, for example, the rudders or even the altimeter ... If something like this is revealed during the investigation of the QZ-8501 flight, the implications of this fact may (but of course not have to) apply to the Polish Tu-154M crash as well.

In our case, it would be about conflicting Poles by awakening political animosities, and thus - breaking up an already divided nation and easier seizure of its material goods - which is what we are observing. So if it was an attack, it was an outside work, which I'm giving to consider to our politicians and investigators, who should also investigate such a possibility (God! - who am I kidding? ...) And the only problem is that in the Republic of Poland III and ½, foreign services are fribbling as they wish, and our rule-misrule plays dumb and pretends that it doesn't know anything. It is enough to mention the shameful case of CIA prisons in Poland ...

But that is a separate matter.

Robert Leśniakiewicz

Chapter 18

For the Fault of the Military:
Mistaken Shootings

In 1896, a glider crashed to the ground in Berlin. Its pilot Otto Lilienthal, after explaining from a scientific point of view how birds fly in the air, died. It was the world's first fatal plane crash ...

On 17 July 2014, the Boeing-777 belonging to Malaysia Airlines crashed in the Donetsk Oblast of Ukraine. All 283 passengers and 15 crew members died. According to the official version, the stratoliner was shot down by a rocket. If this information is confirmed, the July catastrophe will become the largest with the participation of the military, in the history of aviation in the last 50 years. I would like to remind our readers of the plane crashes that arose due to the fault of the military after World War II.

18.1. Fighters and "stray" rockets

On July 23, 1954, Chinese fighters, taking the Hong Kong DC-4 airliner for a reconnaissance plane, shot it down. 10 people were killed.

On June 30, 1962 the greatest catastrophe of that time in the USSR took place - the jetliner Tu-104 about an hour after take-off began to descend quickly and crashed. All 84 people on board died. Later it became clear that at that time the air defense forces unit near Magansk was conducting practice shooting and one of the surface-to-air missiles "got lost" in the storm front, reprogrammed from the training target and hit the plane.

On September 11, 1968, a French SE-210 Caravelle III passenger plane was hit by a surface-to-air missile over the island of Île du Levant lying near Nice where anti-aircraft exercises took place. 95 people died as a result of the disaster.

18.2. Navigational mistakes

On December 21, 1973, Boeing-727 belonging to Libyan airlines, due to a navigational error, headed towards the Israeli airbase on the Sinai Peninsula. Two duty fighters were sent to intercept it. The pilots mistook the machine for an Egyptian plane (at that time the war with Egypt was ongoing) taken over by terrorists. The pilots of the Libyan plane didn't respond to the landing order and the plane was shot down. 216 people died.

On April 20, 1978, the South Korean Boeing-707 deviated from its course, entered USSR airspace over Karelia, and ignored the calls to land from a fighter sent for its interception. As a result, the Soviet Su-15 opened fire on it and the Boeing pilots were forced to land on the surface of Lake Korpijarvi. After the shelling, Boeing lost part of its wing that looked like a rocket on the air defense forces' radars. For its interception, another Su-15 was sent, which shot the target in the air. As a result of the incident, two passengers died.

On June 27, 1980, the Italian DC-9 airliner entered the battlefield of Libyan and NATO air forces over the Tyrrhenian Sea and was destroyed by an air-to-air missile possibly fired by a French fighter. 81 people died.

18.3. Order - destroy the violator!

One of the most famous air crashes involving civil and military aviation took place on the night of August 30/September 1, 1983. The Boeing-747 of South Korean KAL airlines entered the USSR's airspace and was shot down by the Su-15 aircraft. 269 people were killed.

I saw the strange plane flying ahead of me. I'm not a traffic inspector who can detain an intruder and request documents. I was flying behind it to interrupt its flight - recalls the pilot of this fighter Lt. Col. Gennady Osipovich. "The first thing I should do is to make it land. And if it doesn't obey, then stop the flight at all costs. There is simply no other option.

So I got closer and put it in the radar sight. The rocket launch lights came on. Having reached the distance of 13 km from the intruder, I reported - "Target captured - I'm following him, what to do?" Earth replies, "The target has breached the state border. Purpose to destroy."

The first rocket hit the tail - yellow flames appeared. The second one smashed half of the left wing - then the lights and stroboscopes went out.

On June 14, 1993, experts of the International Civil Aviation Organization - ICAO - published a document in which they concluded that the command of the Military Police of the USSR believed that it was issuing an order to shoot down the American RC-135 spy plane, which had previously been observed in the area. And this area was rich in secrets: on

Sakhalin there were six strategic air bases and a naval center, in Kura in Kamchatka there was an ICBM range, and in the Sea of Okhotsk, between Sakhalin and Kamchatka there were nuclear submarines with SLBMs on board. Moreover, it is no coincidence that during the flight of the South Korean jetliner, the American radio reconnaissance satellite Ferret D flew over this region three times, recording all the parameters of the activating communication network of the Soviet air defense forces. Therefore, there is every reason to believe that the Korean Boeing was thrown by the CIA for reconnaissance by fire.[35]

---

[35] Personally, I think that the Russians didn't mean the RC-135 spy plane, but something else, namely the Boeing 707 E-3A Sentry AWACS - a flying command and airspace control station - one of the key links of the SDI/NMD program or Star Wars of President Ronald Reagan, which was also in the Soviet airspace that night, and from which the operations of several radio intelligence planes, the Ferret D satellite and the USS Badger radio-electronic reconnaissance vessel were coordinated. Either way, it was an espionage operation against the USSR and the steps it took were right and justified. See - http://wszechocean.blogspot.com/2013/11/przerwany-rejs.html and http://wszechocean.blogspot.com/2012/12/bieczewninka-zapomniana-baza-okretow.html

18.4. Defense against possible attack

On July 3, 1988, the Iranian Airbus A-300 was shot down by two air-to-water missiles launched from the USS Vincennes anti-aircraft cruiser. 290 passengers and crew members were killed.

Moreover, on August 8, 1988, the same ship, threatening to use weapons, forced another passenger stratoliner flying over the Persian Gulf to change course, which almost led to a collision with another passenger plane ...

Later, the commander of the cruiser declared that the plane hadn't responded to calls and had been identified as an Iranian Air Force F-14 fighter, after which it had been decided to destroy it. US President Ronald Reagan stated that the missiles had been fired as a "defense against an impending attack" in "self-defense".

It is interesting that earlier - in the incident with the South Korean Boeing, flight KAL-007 shot down by the Soviet air defense forces - the Washington administration had expressed amazement at how it had been possible to confuse a passenger plane with a military one.[36]

---

[36] Exactly. I'm curious how it was possible to confuse the radar echo of the large Airbus with the echo of the smaller F-14, which also differ in altitude and other flight parameters? It is obvious that this was either

18.5. Matters in the Caucasus...

On May 9, 1992, the only lucky incident in a series of military air crashes took place - an Armenian Yak-40 passenger plane carrying refugees from Stepanakert to Yerevan was shelled by the Azerbaijani Su-25 attack aircraft, but the crew made a perfect emergency landing. Nobody died, only the plane burned completely.

On September 21, 1993, during the Georgian-Abkhaz conflict, a Georgian liner Tu-134 in the Sukhumi region was shot down from an Abkhazian missile boat. 25 (supposedly even 27 or 28) people died.

The next day, another Georgian Tu-154 airliner was damaged from a missile boat. The pilots managed to land the plane, but unfortunately it fell off the runway and caught fire. 108 people died.

In the evening of the same day, another Tu-154 was shelled during the landing approach, but the rocket missed the target.

---

a neglect/under-training of the cruiser's radar service or a deliberate action. In the context of the latter case, it should be assumed that it was unfortunately a deliberate action.

18.6. Change of target and terrorists

On October 4, 2001, a Russian Tu-154 was shot down by a missile from the S-200 anti-aircraft complex by the Ukrainian Army's air defense forces. 66 passengers and 12 crew members were killed. At the time of the Stratoliner's flight in the region of Feodosia, training and combat exercises of the Ukrainian air defense forces took place there, aimed at teaching the detection and destruction of air targets of a simulated enemy, with the use of surface-to-air anti-aircraft missile systems. Despite the fact that the army officers and the government of Ukraine distanced themselves from this incident, the remains of the plane and the bodies of people traveling by it lifted from the seabed had characteristic holes caused by round bullets, the same with which the warheads of the S-200 missiles are filled. Besides, the difference in time between the explosion of the plane and the missile launch by the Americans in this region matched the time of the missile reaching the target. In the end, the Ukrainian side had to admit that the catastrophe had been caused by the change of automatic targeting from an unmanned target plane to the Russian airliner.

On January 9, 2007, terrorists from the Islamic Army in Iraq shot down a Moldovan An-26 airliner during its flight over Iraqi Baghdad. 34 people were killed.

18.7. My 2 cents

This gloomy list should also include the Polish episode, namely the mysterious and never explained crash of the PLL LOT An-24 plane, side number SP-LTF, flight LO-165, which happened on April 2, 1969 near Polica summit in the High Beskids. 53 people died then - passengers and crew members. And this is how I wrote about it in "Echo Jordanowa".

This catastrophe is also shrouded in a thick veil of mystery. The journalist of Gazeta Krakowska, editor Jerzy Pałosz, who investigated this case believed that after the collapse of communism in Poland, he would be able to reach witnesses and documents without any obstacles. It soon turned out that the witnesses didn't say much, and most of the documents were still in the safes of the Ministry of Interior and Administration, the Ministry of National Defense and the Institute of National Remembrance, and there was no chance of their immediate declassification. This case resembles the Angleton "jungle of mirrors", tracks intersect and sometimes exclude each other, while the reflections blind and confuse ... (=> J. Pałosz - "Tragedia pod Zawoją" in "Gazeta Krakowska" of April 10, 1994, p. 6 and 7, and of April 11-12, 1994, p. 3) One thing is certain that the then authorities of the Polish People's Republic did everything in their power to silence the matter of this catastrophe and wring its neck. The truth was too inconvenient ... [...]

There are several hypotheses as to the causes of the tragedy near Zawoja:

1. Hijacking the plane and fleeing to Austria;

2. Downing of the plane by the Czechoslovak air defense forces;

3. Error of the pilots who, after flying over Cracow, tried to turn the plane back and, due to a navigational error, hit Polica slope;

4. Error of the ground service of the Krakow-Balice airport, which observed the Li-2 plane (flying in front of the SP-LTF) and provided the data on which the An-24 pilots relied;

5. Influence of other factors beyond the control of people: disastrous weather conditions, technical errors, failures of navigation systems, etc.

Either way, each of these causes led to the An-24 crashing on Polica slope at 4:07 pm on April 2, 1969. 53 people died then. Nobody survived. Editor Pałosz in his article, asks the key question regarding the case: what caught the attention of the LO-165 crew in the Jędrzejów area, that they missed the marker there and took the next marker of the Krakow airport - Balice for it? Nobody answered this question.

The ufological hypothesis that I put forward once assumes that on April 2, 1969, the PLL LOT An-24 cruise plane, flight number LO-165, which simply crashed as a result of a navigational mistake made by the radar operator from the Kraków-Balice airport, confused by a visible on the radar screen echo of some plane flying over ... Skawina! It could have been a UFO, of course, but... The flight controller was giving commands to this object, and the crew of LO-165 flying 40 km further south followed them. The effect of this, in the then hideous April weather, could be only one - the plane crashed several dozen meters below the main peak of Polica ... [...]

An interesting hypothesis was put forward by one of the experts on plane crashes and lawyer Mariusz Fryckowski. He said that the plane could have a bomb (or a similar device) on board and its operation caused the plane's loss, or it was shot down with an anti-tank rifle (gunfire). The idea is interesting because no one took it into account and no one looked for signs of a weapon that could fire 7.92 mm caliber bullets (Polish model 35 anti-tank rifle, also called Uruguay, with a range of 300 - 500 m) or 14.5 mm (Soviet PTRD or PTRS, with a range of 500-800 m), which, however, were withdrawn from the Polish Armed Forces and couldn't be used against this aircraft. However, these rifles are experiencing a certain renaissance. Since the 1980s, many armies of the world have introduced the so-called "Large-caliber sniper rifles" AMR (Anti Materiel Rifle) - a rifle for destroying technical equipment with a caliber 50, or 12.7 mm], the concept of which is partly derived from anti-tank rifles - they are used for precise destruction of light equipment from long distances[37]. Anyway - this issue is still unsolved.[38]

Yuri Danilov

---

[37] See - http://grzybypl.blogspot.com/2013/04/44-lata-temu-na-policy.html

[38] Text and photos – „Tajny XX wieka" no. 36/2014, p. 12-13

Chapter 19

Seven theories of the disappearance of the flight MH-370

There are seven main theories about what could have happened to the Boeing 777, flight MH-370 that mysteriously disappeared somewhere in the airspace of Asia or the Indian Ocean on March 8, 2014.

Theory no. 1. THE SINISTER ACTION OF DEAD PILOTS:

FOR: Why do we suspect pilots? The plane's transponder stopped sending signals to air traffic control and other airborne machines at the most convenient time: during switching from communication with air traffic control in Malaysia to air traffic control in Vietnam.

AGAINST: The idea that the pilots used the plane to kill themselves as well as the crew and passengers is unacceptable and would be some taboo for aviation, but it cannot be ruled out.

Theory No. 2. - THE SEIZURE BY TERRORISTS

FOR: This theory was most popular when it turned out that there were two Iraqis on board - one 18-year-old and other 28-year-old, who were traveling with stolen passports.

AGAINST: So far, no terrorist group has admitted to hijacking this plane, and the special services haven't observed any activity in terrorist circles related to the skyjacking of this plane.

Theory No. 3 - SUDDEN DISASTER

FOR: Aviation and plane crash specialists first suggested that something sudden and terrible had happened, such as an on-board bomb explosion, or a failure of the engine or machine structure.

AGAINST: If that were the case, the debris would have been found near the point where the transponder had been turned off.

Theory No. 4 - BOARD FIRE

FOR: An electrical fire or a flammable cargo fire would be able to switch off communications equipment and prevent the crew and passengers from calling for help.

AGAINST: Of course it is possible, but the crew and passengers would have time to get into the cockpit and regain control of the plane.

Theory No. 5. - DECOMPRESSION

FOR: Slow or fast decompression causing oxygen loss would have killed anyone on board.

AGAINST: But even in that case - as aviation experts say - if the anoxia killed everyone on board, the autopilot would have still flown the plane to Beijing and the aircraft would have been seen on the radar.

Theory No. 6 - HIDING OF THE PLANE

FOR: There is a possibility that someone did land the plane at some distant airport and hid it from the world.

AGAINST: But why would someone have gone to so much trouble to steal a passenger plane? Skyjacking a transport plane would have been much easier ...

Theory No. 7 - ACCIDENTAL DOWNING

FOR: The civilian plane may have been shot down mistakenly by the military.

AGAINST: There is no evidence that flight MH-370 was shot down by the army.

Mark Diamat (AP)

Chapter 20

End of the mystery of the flight MH-370?

At the beginning of August this year, world media reported that fragments of the Boeing 777, flight MH-370, which had mysteriously disappeared on March 8, 2014, during the flight between Kuala Lumpur and Beijing, were found on the island of Réunion. Onet.pl writes about it:

Special beach cleaning teams found an element approximately two meters long in the vicinity of Saint-André. It is most likely a fragment of the wing. It is heavily overgrown with seaweed and shells, which indicates a long stay in the water.

French authorities launched an investigation to determine the plane to which belongs the fragment found. So far, three hypotheses have been formulated. It could be a piece of the wing of a plane that crashed near Reunion in May 2006, a piece of the Yemeni Airbus A310 that crashed in June 2009 near the Comoros archipelago, or the Malaysian Boeing that went missing over the Indian Ocean in March 2014.

The latter option is not excluded by aviation safety expert Xavier Tytelman, quoted by the AFP agency.

The disappearance of the Malaysian Boeing 777 is still one of the greatest secrets of modern aviation. The Malaysia Airlines aircraft disappeared from radar on March 8, 2014.

The Boeing 777 with 239 people on board, flying to Beijing vanished from radar on March 8, less than an hour after taking off from the airport in the Malaysian capital, Kuala Lumpur. Of the 239 people on board, 153 were citizens of the People's Republic of China. Among the passengers was a group of prominent Chinese calligraphers returning from an exhibition in Kuala Lumpur.

The search for the Malaysian aircraft is the largest operation of this type in the history of aviation.

According to Australian experts, the Boeing 777 of the Malaysian airlines was flown by the autopilot before it hit the ocean. At that time, most likely the entire crew and passengers - 239 people in total - were already dead. It was hypothesized that the machine was depressurized and the plane was moving in one of the air corridors until the fuel ran out. (RZ)

Today we know with certainty that these and other remains belong to the Boeing 777, flight MH-370. And we also know for sure that they would have been found sooner had it not been for the South India Junk Ocean Whirl, a current system that traps huge amounts of plastic packaging and other debris, among which the plastic pieces of the Boeing 777, which crashed into water, drowned when it fell, depleted of fuel, into the Indian Ocean, somewhere west of Australia.

Of course, we don't know what happened on the plane. One of the versions says about the depressurization of the cabin and the almost immediate death of the crew and passengers, and the plane, let loose, was flying towards Antarctica. We do know one thing, however, and that is that the plane crashed into the South Indian or West Australian Ocean Current. Its heavier remains went to the bottom, and the lighter or air-filled ones began to drift counterclockwise initially towards the equator, then west towards the Comoros, where they were found.

The Indian Ocean and its system of ocean currents. It is here that is located one of the five ocean plastic dumps that delayed the discovery of the remains of the plane of the fateful flight MH-370 ...[39]

Nevertheless, the last 8 hours of flight of this machine and what happened on board are a secret. I'm only sure about one thing - flight MH-370 was not carried by aliens to another planet ...

Robert Leśniakiewicz

---

[39] We deal with a similar plastic problem in several places of the World Ocean - see "Wszechocean: stan klęski rozumu 1-3" http://wszechocean.blogspot.com/2012/03/wszechocean-stan-kleski-rozumu-1.html "Plastykowego koszmaru ciąg dalszy - http://wszechocean.blogspot.com/2014/09/plastykowy-problem-koszmaru-ciag-dalszy.html, "Raport ONZ" - http://wszechocean.blogspot.com/2015/04/raport-onz-nasze-oceany-sa-zasmiecone.html. This applies to littering the so-called Hawaiian Whirlpool - a body of water located between Hawaii, California and Alaska. The same is true of the Indian Ocean, where masses of plastic debris from Australia and Africa circulate, carried by the Mozambique, South Indian, West Australian and South Equatorial Currents to the launch site. And it is because of this litter, among other things, that it was not possible to find floating fragments of the Boeing 777 fuselage before ...

Chapter 21

Kaczyński was killed by the Americans themselves: Operation "Red Rose"

A few days ago I found the following text on the Internet on Facebook, which is a voice in the discussion on the catastrophe of April 10, 2010, in which many prominent Polish people died, including the presidential couple - Lech and Maria Kaczyński. Here is this text:

The following translation has already appeared on several blogs and websites. I'm posting it here, because the discussion about the Smolensk attack is still heated (and it should be so). All committees, as well as independent "researchers" only add fuel to the fire, obscuring the image of the matter with new "facts" and theories.

There are a number of reservations to the following text, such as the fact that it doesn't explain some important things, for example the complete rupture of the plane's fuselage. It also doesn't answer the question of whether all the people who were supposed to fly with the President were on board. I emphasize once again that I don't believe that after the CASA crash a few years ago (which I believe was also an attack), Polish officers boarded the plane with the President and so many people holding the highest positions in the country.

To many questions, nobody even tries to answer. One of them is: who handed over the red rose exactly one month before the Smolensk attack? The incident called "the rose bombing" is very shadowy, especially since the rose was handed to Kaczyński by a person wearing a skullcap, as if he had wanted to manifest his Jewish affiliation. The symbolism in this case seems very suspicious.

Has anyone reverted to the topic of the English-speaking individual allegedly being in the control tower? What happened to the lights at the airport that they were replaced so carefully after the crash? There are hundreds of such questions.

The misdirection with GPS could be one of the elements of the attack - the actions of the secret services differ from amateurishness in that they are thought out to be 100 percent successful. Remember that the US is no longer ruled by the Americans - both the government and all government agencies, health care, military, education etc. are in the hands of the Bolsheviks - the same people who murdered tens of millions of Christians in Russia and elsewhere.

The Russian services explained how L. Kaczyński was killed. The crash of the presidential Tu-154M resulted from a malicious reorientation of the American satellite system installed on the plane. Consequently, the pilot didn't have time to react in bad weather and pull the plane out of the fall. (...)

When inspecting the site of the fall, specialists were most surprised why the plane deviated from the flight path by as much as 500 meters and was only 5 meters above the ground, instead of 60. According to experts, the Americans locally changed the ground level in the aircraft's GPS system. Nobody, except the US secret services, is able to locally change the GPS coordinates.

This possibility turned out to be useful during the war. For example, in the period of Georgia's attack on South Ossetia in 2008, Russian artillerymen faced the problem of a shift in the public GPS signal. The Americans moved the coordinates 300 meters in this zone. As a result, Russian artillerymen couldn't use the generally available GPS system. This thesis was confirmed when government Hummers with backup drives for insertion into GPS devices on board were seized on the Georgian side.[40]

21.1. My 2 cents

Is something like this possible? First, after reading this text, I shrugged my shoulders - just one more theory hatched in some unboiled head, another one would like to have his moment in history and he came up with a theory that will soon be forgotten because is ridiculous. By the way, the hypothesis about manipulating GPS indications appeared in the investigation at the very beginning and ... quickly disappeared, replaced by the screams of "genetic" Polish "patriots" as well as "theories" of various "specialists", including from the USA, brought by Antoni Macierewicz.

---

[40]

https://www.facebook.com/photo.php?fbid=1052647818095131&set=a.225802674112987.76779.100000497674545&type=1&theater

I changed this view when I remembered the events of September 2010, when I was on vacation in Międzyzdroje. For a week, we traveled here and there, exploring everything that could be explored, and seeing everything that could be seen. A typical tourist and sightseeing trip, which we completed in 90% despite quite nasty, windy and rainy weather. But is it related to the crash of the government "tutka"?

Well, it is. When traveling around the islands, I used on-board GPS navigation that I had installed in my car. One day I noticed that - ATTENTION! - GPS indications didn't coincide with what I experienced in the field. The difference was even 100-250 m! Back then, I explained it with the terrain configuration and the possibility of big amount of meteoric iron remaining underground ... I described the matter on the website - http://wszechocean.blogspot.com/2012/08/podroz-uczona-do-polskiej-atlantydy-1.html and others.

I had a second case recently in Slovakia. I was driving from Dolný Kubín to Trstená. Passing by the Templar castle in Oravský Podzámok, I was surprised to notice that my GPS navigator "went crazy" and gave some strange altitude indications. For 2-3 minutes I had some strange readings varying by up to 100 meters. I blamed it on solar activity, some kind of magnetic storm, or satellite signal interference, and forgot about it. Until yesterday.

Does this have anything to do with the Polish plane crash? I don't know if it was so, but if it was, it could have. Indication of altitude above sea level of GPS is irrelevant in the case of a car moving in a two-dimensional plane, but of colossal importance in the case of an aircraft moving in three-dimensional space! Such an attack could have been carried out and would have been extremely effective - the target would have been destroyed.

Let's look at the circumstances of this catastrophe: limited visibility - fog over the airport. Perfect weather just for such an operation confusing pilots who until the end believed the instruments without paying attention to any alarms - that desperate: TERRAIN AHEAD, TERRAIN AHEAD and PULL UP! PULL UP! ...

Only the fundamental question remained: cui bono, cui prodest? Who wanted to kill the Polish president and his companions? Personally, I'm convinced that if it was an attack, its target was not so much the presidential couple or the notable accompanying them, but all Poles who got even more divided by this crime. And that was the point, to make Poles get at each other's throats, while the perpetrators of the attack stood aside and took more benefits from it. In this respect, the technique of manipulating people's minds reminds me of the operations of this type carried out by the CIA in the banana republics, of which level was reached by Poland after 1989.

I think this is also an explanation of what happened to the Malaysian plane that mysteriously disappeared somewhere over one of the oceans on March 8, 2014. Now it seems to be clarified - since you can enter incorrect data into specific GPS receivers, someone could confuse the flight crew of the MH370 and QZ-8501 and lead the machine to, devil knows where, in conditions of poor visibility: night, storm, fog ... And if a saboteur was on board ... In a word - this hypothesis explains a lot.

Robert Leśniakiewicz

Chapter 22

The mystery of the missing Boeing

Exactly one year has passed since the missing of the Malaysian Boeing-777, flight MH-370, going from Kuala Lumpur to Beijing. The search for the plane with 277 passengers and 12 crew members on board hasn't led to anything so far ...

22.1. A victim of a psychopath

The huge metal bird disappeared completely ... Even the satellite couldn't find any trace of it. Hypotheses have multiplied during this year, and new versions of events are being considered over and over again. What could really have happened there?

From the beginning, the main assumption was that the plane was hijacked by the first pilot named Zaharie Ahmad Shah. Why? Apparently, he was severely depressed due to a stormy divorce from his wife and was also dissatisfied with the sentence in another court case. As a result, the pilot fell into a rage and skyjacked the plane with passengers. The plane lost communication with the dispatchers because the pilot turned off the transponder - the device that maintains this communication.

Such a hypothesis was presented by a New Zealander - Evan Wilson - a former pilot and founder of the Kivi Airlines airline company. Wilson published an entire book containing his guesses but the experts dismissed them. The point is, Wilson hasn't provided any convincing evidence for this, and besides, why would the pilot have commited suicide in such a complex manner?[41]

---

[41] And yet pilots have used planes several times as a suicide tool, as evidenced by the Germanwings Airbus A320 crash in the French Alps

22.2. Al-Qaeda girl?

Therefore, a second similar hypothesis was put forward - the plane became the victim not of the first pilot, but of the copilot - also a psychopath who broke up with his girlfriend. Fariq Abdul Hamid allegedly locked himself in the cockpit and did his dark work there. But again, a miss: in fact, he had no reason to commit suicide, just the opposite - he was going to get married and took care of his job. Incidentally, Fariq simply loved life: he used to invite beautiful girls to the cockpit. And he was the last person to establish radio contact with the air traffic controllers in that cockpit. And what if there was a girl there? Considering that the plane was headed for Beijing, it can be assumed that such a girl may have been a member of the Chinese branch of Al-Qaeda, and it was she who played a sinister role ...

22.3. Landing on the island

in March 2015. In this case, the suicide pilot suffered from depression and burnout syndrome. In desperation, he directed the machine to the mountain slope and killed himself and 149 passengers and crew. See S. Bednarz & R. Leśniakiewicz - "Tajemnice katastrof lotniczych", Jordanów 2019

So experts are considering the possibility of a terrorist attack. Here are the possible variants. The most interesting one sounds like this: there were terrorists on board the plane who took control of the cockpit and intended to direct the plane to some skyscraper in the capital city, as it had been in New York. On the other hand, it is known that the plane turned and flew back to Kuala Lumpur, which would mean that the terrorists were going to crash into a double skyscraper in the Malayan capital, for example.[42]

So? According to the authors of the hypothesis, the entire action was planned and carried out by MOSSAD in order to blame Iran for the attack.[43]

Or maybe everything was different? The criminals took control of the plane, turned off the transponder and intended to unnoticeably land the machine somewhere on an island away from civilization, and then use it for their own purposes. And

---

[42] Two Petronas Towers, 452 m each, for comparison Twin Towers WTC 1 was 417 m, and WTC 2 - 415 m

[43] This hypothesis makes sense because Malaysia has no relations with Israel and doesn't allow citizens of this country to enter its territory, hence the thought that it was some kind of Jewish retaliation, but would it have been effective? - rather not, and on the contrary, as anti-Semitic moods in Arab countries would have intensified and it would have worsened relations with Israel even further.

British sportswoman Catherine Tee, who was traveling by yacht with her husband in this area and at the same time, saw the Chinese navy at sea - and a plane flying very low. According to her version, the people who took over the plane intended - like kamikaze - to hit one of the Chinese ships.

22.4. Shocking hypotheses

A shadow was cast also on Russia. For example, the American journalist Jeff Wise assumed that the plane was taken over by the Russian special services and landed secretly in Kazakhstan. That the hijackers reprogrammed the apparatus so that the air traffic controllers received false information about the direction of flight at the time the liner was heading to Baikonur. But what for? Wise tried to answer.

An even more shocking hypothesis appeared on some websites: the MH-370 flight turned out to be exactly the same plane that had crashed over... Ukraine! And it was the work of the CIA agents. They hijacked the plane to Amsterdam, named it MH-17, and then sent it back to Kuala Lumpur via the Donetsk Oblast, where it was shot down by US special forces to discredit Russia. But the question arises: why is it all so complicated?

This entire Ukrainian version only answers the question: where did the plane depart? He was shot down and the remains were collected. The hypotheses formulated don't give any answer. After all, nothing was left of the stratoliner! If the cause was a technical malfunction and the plane simply exploded, or flew until it ran out of fuel, then it or its remains would have been found. Maybe it fell into the Marian Trench? After all, no one knows where this stratoliner was taken. Or maybe someone knows, but will never say ...?[44]

So there is nothing else to do but believe the most incredible hypothesis - MH-370 was hijacked by aliens! ...[45]

Yelena Galanova

---

[44] This article was written in August 2015, before the wreckage of the MH-370 aircraft was found in Mauritius and other Indian Ocean islands. So there could be no aliens, and it was a "normal" plane crash, the causes of which are still extremely unclear!

[45] Text and ilustrations – „Tajny XX wieka" no 13/2015, p. 3

Chapter 23

Helios 522 and MH-370 - analogies?

The crash of the Helios Airways Boeing 737-31S Reg. No. 5B-DBY, flight HA522 from Larnaca (LCA) to Athens (ATH) happened on August 14, 2005, near the capital of Greece - Athens - more precisely on the slope of Grammatikos hill - N38°13'53"-E23°58'12". All 121 people on board died at 12:04 PM EEST/09:04 AM GMT.

The cause of the crash was most likely an unfortunate coincidence, related to the error of engineers during service work on the machine on the ground and the pilots misinterpreting the alarm signal, triggered by decompression during the climb. As a result, passengers and the crew lost consciousness. The plane deprived of control was doomed to a collision with the ground, which took place 3 hours after take-off.

Only when the second black box was found, it was sent back to France for analysis, in the hope of helping to determine the causes of the crash. As it turned out, the device worked properly during the flight, which after the accident made it possible to read the data on the course of the flight and the record of the voices in the crew cabin.

Meticulous tests confirmed the suspicion that the switch controlling the oxygen pressure equalizing system was mistakenly left by the mechanics servicing the machine in the morning before the flight in the "manual" position instead of "auto". The "auto" position in normal flight is responsible for the consistent change in oxygen pressure as flight altitude changes in order to provide sufficient oxygen for passengers and crew inside the cabin. In the "manual" position, the cockpit doesn't maintain a constant oxygen pressure by itself and must be monitored by the pilots. Otherwise, as the altitude increases, the available oxygen gradually decreases, leading to decompression and fainting of the people inside the airplane. Unfortunately, the pilots misinterpreted the alarm signal that was triggered due to decompression in the passenger cabin of the plane, and continued the climb. Already after a dozen or so minutes, due to hypoxia, they lost consciousness and despite establishing communication with the ground control trying to help, they could no longer perform any actions that could save the plane from a crash.

The first problems arose at 10.30am, when attempts to contact Eleftherios Venizelos airport failed. After a few minutes, the pilots reported problems to the Larnaca base, and this was the last contact with the plane. The scheduled 10:45 am stopover in Athens didn't take place, and in response to this, two F-16 fighters were sent to investigate the situation. At 11:18 am, the F-16 pilots managed to establish eye contact with the Boeing - they discovered unconscious pilots at the controls of the plane. The catastrophe seemed only a matter of time. For some time, the plane remained in the air thanks to the autopilot, which, due to the lack of response of the crew, kept it above the Athens airport. In fact, it only delayed the annihilation. Some time later the fighter pilots noticed a moving person in the cockpit. The man seemed to be trying to take control of the machine. Subsequent DNA testing of bodies found in the cockpit revealed that flight attendant Andreas Prodromous entered the cockpit and attempted to bring the plane to the ground. Today it is known how it happened that one person remained conscious while both pilots, the rest of the crew and all passengers were unconscious. An oxygen generator that powers the masks, which automatically appear above all seats in the plane after exceeding the ceiling of about 3,000 meters in the event of decompression, works only for several minutes. The flight attendant, on the other hand, used a portable oxygen cylinder (there are 4 such cylinders on board) and thus remained fully conscious. In addition, he was a professional diver and a special forces soldier, so his body was better adapted to work in such extreme conditions. At the time when the brave man was calling for help on the radio with a weak voice of "mayday", he tried to revive the 2nd pilot and take over the controls - the left engine went out due to lack of fuel. Then the plane banked to the left side and crashed to the ground near Grammatikos Hill at 12:04 pm EEST.

Among the 121 victims (115 passengers + 6 crew members) were 104 Cypriots, 12 Greeks, a family of four from Armenia and a German pilot. Coroner Philippos Koutsaftis confirming the deaths of individual victims of the crash stated beyond any doubt that at the time of the plane's impact with the ground all 121 people aboard the Boeing 737 were still alive. (Wikipedia)

They were alive, that's true, but even if they had survived the catastrophe, they would have been vegetables due to anoxia ... It also reminds me of the mysterious plane crash in 1983, which the Polish press wrote about - the Learjet 25 catastrophe mentioned here which happened in May 1983.

More information on this outrageous topic was obtained by Mr. Stanisław Bednarz, who specializes in the history of air accidents and disasters, who found on the Internet the note from AP of 20 May 1983, which reads as follows:

23.1. German Learjet: the empty cockpit - a disaster in the Atlantic?

London, AP, May 19 - West German service jet deviated from a course of 1,600 mi/~ 2,560 km on Wednesday, on a training flight from Vienna, and no one from air traffic control could believe that it crashed in the Atlantic, 200 mi/320 km south of Iceland.

United States officials in Iceland theorized that the in-flight oxygen system had failed, causing the three-man crew to become unconscious. Officials said the pilots probably had died in the crash. The search for the wreckage of the plane was canceled early today.

As the plane flew over northern Europe, British, Dutch and American fighters were sent for interception due to fears that there would be a disaster in a populated area, but the plane flew in a straight line over Scotland and further over the Atlantic at an altitude of about 43,000 ft/~14,330 m.

Two RAF Phantom fighters caught up with it over Scotland, and RAF John Marr, the pilot of one of them, said that there was definitely no one in the cockpit. He also thought that there could have been some incident and that the crew might have been lying on board.

One theory is that the oxygen delivery system inside the plane broke down and the crew turned on the autopilot, and the pilots left the cockpit to perform an expansion test.

Harry Hopkins, a member of the British Flight Safety Committee, said that the biggest secret was the empty space in the cockpit.

"In most emergencies, one pilot is allowed to leave his seat while the other tries to fly a plane," he said.

Officials said the Learjet 25B aircraft, owned by the Federal Republic of Germany charter company, departed Vienna on Wednesday at around 3:00 pm CEST for a 450 mi/720 km flight to Hamburg, West Germany. It had fuel for 4 hours of flight. The Learjet 25B has a top cruising speed of almost 550 mph/~ 885 km/h.

Manfred Kuppers, Chief Inspector of the Federal Office of West German Aviation in Braunschweig, said radio contact broke off 40 minutes after take-off, when the plane was 12 mi/19 km north of Nuremberg. He said the plane flew over the west of the Netherlands and disappeared from radar screens over the North Sea about 250 mi/400 km northwest of Scotland.

Lieutenant Commander William Clyde, spokesman for the US NATO base in Keflavik, Iceland, said the crew was absent and he was fairly certain the oxygen shortage was caused by a malfunction in the aircraft's oxygen delivery system. He also said the plane probably crashed after running out of fuel.

Dr John Lemon, a doctor at the UK's Civil Aviation Authority, said the symptoms of hypoxia include blurred vision, finger tremors and sleepiness. He also said the condition can come so slowly that the person may not realize that something is wrong.

James Greenwood, vice president of Learjet plant in Tucson, AZ said that until the unit was recovered it would be premature to infer what had gone wrong.

"Any speculation about what happened would be pure speculation at this point."[46]

Don't both of these events remind us of something?

They do - the Malaysian Boeing 777, flight MH370, which went missing somewhere in the Indian Ocean on March 8,

---

[46] „The New York Times" -
http://www.nytimes.com/1983/05/20/world/german-learjet-cockpit-empty-is-thought-to-crash-in-the-atlantic.html

2014, and now the Egyptian Airbus 320, which fell into the Mediterranean Sea about 290-300 km north of Alexandria.

Both the Cypriot Boeing 737 and the German Learjet depressurized, resulting in the crew and passengers first falling into a coma and then dying from lack of oxygen. This is a certainty and there is nothing to discuss. The question that should now be asked is: was this the case with the missing Malaysian Airlines Boeing 777?

Note that in the case of the MH370 and MS804, the planes, after losing communication, performed some unforeseen by flight plan, strange maneuvers, which in the case of MH370 ended with a permanent change of course and a flight somewhere in the southern sectors of the Indian Ocean on the way to Antarctica, and in the case of MS804 - the flight to the sea.

On the other hand, the German Learjet and the Cypriot Boeing 737 interrupted communication and continued to fly being led by the autopilot until the fuel ran out. It appears that the crew and passengers lost consciousness quickly - except for the Boeing 737 flight attendant who attempted to bring the machine down to the ground but he failed and it ended in disaster.

Therefore, I think that it could have been similar with the Malaysian Boeing 777, which was de-pressurized - we don't know why, maybe there was a bomb on board, a technical defect or an object hitting the plane - which then made a left turn by 90°, passed over Sumatra and turned 90° left again - this time flying over the Indian Ocean towards Antarctica ... Perhaps, as in the case of flight HA522, there was someone on board who tried to return the plane to Kuala Lumpur, but didn't have enough knowledge or just strength to do it ...

Summing up: the explanation of the Egyptian Airbus accident may be helpful in explaining the Malaysian Boeing 777 crash. The similarity of all four accidents is obvious and for now - until the remains of these planes are recovered - we only have hypotheses. Even as exotic as the work of the sinister forces of the Bermuda Triangle (What does that have to do with the price of tea in China?), extremely nasty aliens (are our planes interfering with their flying?), terrorists (after all, there will always be some freak) or megacryometeorites who fly as they please.

Another piece of information about a plane crash of this type - January 10 - Cessna 441 en route from Shreveport to Baton Rouge, Louisiana, interrupts communication and goes far out to sea, of course led by autopilot, and eventually falls into the Atlantic Ocean off the coast of North Carolina due to the lack of fuel. Two passengers, New Louisiana State University soccer coach Bo Rein, and the pilot died. It is assumed that they became unconscious in flight due to hypoxia resulting from cockpit decompression. (Hades)

Robert Leśniakiewicz

Chapter 24

Flight MH-370: The Man Who Didn't Give Up

It would seem that the mysterious disappearance of the Malaysian Boeing 777, flight MH-370 will disappear from the media, pushed aside by ever newer news. And yet it won't. A few days ago, I received an email from my French friend from Singapore - Mr. Patrick Moncelet, who wrote to me about an extraordinary man who is still looking for traces of the catastrophe:

He is an unusual man: Blaine Gibson - he writes in his email - you must have heard of him. He is a US prosecutor who is still looking for the wreckage of the MH-370 washed ashore in several East African countries, Réunion, Madagascar, etc. He has found an entire collection of them. Many were positively identified as being from this Boeing 777 or others, and they are now examined diligently I suppose.

The "official" search of 120,000 km2 of the southern Indian Ocean was finished early and the chances of finding the wreckage were reduced. It would seem that the plane fell to the northern so-called "arc" - as long as the Imarsat data is correct, because we have to remember that something like this plane has been seen on the Maldives' atolls - I think you know that story.

In this whole saga, I think the most scandalous is attitude of the Malaysian government: they hardly cared whether the plane was found or not, and the Prime Minister didn't even offer Gibson financial aid, so he has to continue the search with his own money - it's unbelievable…!

Reading this introduction about Mr. Gibson, I also learned that he is a friend of Peter Davenport - that's right! - The guy who runs National UFO Reporting in Washington. Anyway, Mr. Gibson is also interested in UFOs and the explosion that happened, as you know, in 1908 in the Tunguska region of Siberia - he was even there to investigate it in situ! (I also did long research on the same event.) So we have the brave Mr. Gibson who promises not to stop his search until he explains the fate of this plane. I greet him!

Incidentally, there must have been an explosion on board - most likely caused by 200 kg lithium batteries, which made the captain panic, and he tried to turn back, but set the autopilot to a course for … Maldives or somewhere in the Indian Ocean - who knows? What is most amazing is the lack of any machine remains in the so-called "arc" despite intense searches. But many of them were found on the islands of the Indian Ocean and in East Africa. Finding some of them can be explained by the action of sea winds and currents, but then why have they not been seen in the open ocean? After all, there should have been many of them.

Best regards!

Patrick Moncelet

Exactly - this is the most puzzling of it all. Here's an article from the Yahoo Finance website about Mr. Gibson:

Canberra, Australia, AP - His fedora, bomber pilot's leather jacket and manner resembles Indiana Jones. That's what looks like Blaine Gibson, who didn't achieve such a triumph as the film hero looking for the legendary chest with tablets containing the Ten Commandments. And he doesn't even try it.

Ark of the Covenant, I didn't find it. However, I believe it is somewhere in Ethiopia, Gibson recently told an AP journalist. This amateur explorer wants to solve the latest mystery - the disappearance of the Malaysian flight MH-370. He is the first person looking for this plane to find any traces of it, and says he won't let go until he finds a solution to the mystery.

"I have always liked to travel, but I have always liked to travel for some purpose, and now solving the mystery of the MH-370 flight is such a goal ... - until someone else or I find out what happened to that plane and the people on board," he said during his visit to the search headquarters in Canberra, Australia.

Boeing-777, carrying 227 passengers and 12 crew members, is believed to have plunged into the South Indian Ocean after the uninterrupted and unrealized flight from Kuala Lumpur, Malaysia to Beijing, China, on March 8, 2014.

The first reports that Gibson found the debris of the plane were met with skepticism. Other pieces of the plane fragments were found entirely by accident. But how is it possible that one "private citizen" found the wreckage of the plane, and not an army of rescuers during an expensive and multinational search? Answer: No official search has been carried out outside the body of water with an area of 46,000 sq. miles/120,000 km² of ocean floor SW of Australia, which was recognized as the crash site.

But the triangular panel that Gibson found on February 27 was confirmed as an almost obvious horizontal stabilizer from the wing of the MH-370 aircraft.

Gibson said he ended up in Mozambique in part because oceanographers told him the plane's wreckage might have been carried there, in part because he had never been to the country. (58-year-old California-born Gibson has already been to 177 countries, and he would like to visit all countries.) Having met relatives of the missing, he ended the chances of finding anything during his search.

"It was good management, but also a lot of luck," said Gibson. "Many beaches in Réunion and Mauritius and other parts of the world have been searched to no effect."

Gibson found 13 pieces of possible remains in Madagascar with the help of local residents with whom he befriended. He and the victims' families were frustrated by the Malaysians' reluctance to search for, collect, and investigate the plane's debris. Gibson delivered 5 pieces of the plane for the meeting of the families of flight MH-370 passengers on September 12 in Canberra with officials from the Australian Transport Safety Bureau who were conducting deep-sea sonar surveys on behalf of Malaysia.

Warren Truss, the former vice-prime minister who oversaw the search before retiring from politics in February this year, expects more of Gibson's findings to be confirmed.

"He obviously did an excellent job for this search," said Truss.

Australian oceanographer David Griffin - one of the two whose clues put Gibson in the right direction, noted that the American was frustrated that responsibility had fallen into a gap that divided the agencies coordinating the search.

"He sees that one man can do the job. I think it's scary that someone with the capacity and resources can just get on with it," Griffin said.

Gibson was also a volunteer archaeologist in Belize and Guatemala researching the fate of the Mayan civilization. His old friend Peter Davenport said he wasn't surprised this brawler was so completely caught up in this aviation secrecy. Davenport who is director of NUFORC in Washington state, said he had once gotten Gibson interested in the event in Tunguska: a gigantic explosion near the Podkamennaya Tunguska in Siberia that devastated vast forests in 1908.

"The next thing I know he wanted to do was to befriend people who knew something about this event and get to the heart of this mystery, which I still think remains a mystery. Clearly it wasn't a meteor," said Davenport. (Gibson concluded that it was a meteor that evaporated in the atmosphere.)

Davenport said of his friend that for at least two decades he has had the opportunity to solve these puzzles and mysteries and he desires it.

"He's very committed to it, he gets along with many people, he's non-confrontational, I could say he's got such abilities that people want to work with him and help him," says Davenport.

Gibson said he has always worked on his travels and even sold his deceased parents' home in Carmel, CA for a little more than a million dollars in 2014, which became capital for his search for the MH-370 plane.

But he and the families of the victims would like governments to coordinate efforts to collect airplane fragments washed ashore in the western Indian Ocean. Research on debris could explain the crash and model their drift, which in turn would make it easier to find the location of the main wreckage mass. The underwater search will end around December, if no new premises are found to determine the site of the crash.

Gibson doesn't know where he will look further, but the Seychelles and Comoros are still unexplored. He doesn't have any distinguished theory about what happened and cautions against publicly accepting the most popular hypothesis that Captain Zaharie Ahmad Shah hijacked the plane.

"People choose without thinking this hypothesis because there is no other explanation. It is very easy to relate it to the pilot who cannot defend himself, write about the secret and finish the search: this is unacceptable," he said.

He also said that the missing plane is a global problem that could be unraveled by the work of many nations.

"We need to know when getting on the plane that it will not disappear with us," he added.[47]

Robert Leśniakiewicz

---

[47] Yahoo Finance - http://finance.yahoo.com/news/mh370-wreckage-hunter-wont-until-mystery-solved-025900469.html

Chapter 25

Boeing 777, flight MH 370 flew towards Antarctica

Malaysia Airlines Boeing-777, flight number MH370 flew towards Antarctica. In this mysterious story which happened four years ago, we have a new twist: the Boeing-777 flew towards Antarctica. This conclusion was reached by specialists who analyzed the data from the satellites. The stratoliner made three left turns, took a course westward toward Antarctica, and continued to fly for several more hours after communication with it was lost.

We remind you that the passengers of the Boeing-777 flight MH-370 were traveling from Kuala Lumpur to Beijing and disappeared from the radar screens on the night of March 8, 2014. There were 227 passengers from 14 countries and 12 crew members on board. It is assumed that the crash took place in the southern Indian Ocean, but to this day no traces of the plane have been found. As "The New Zealand Herald" wrote with reference to the well-known international expert Malcolm Brenner, people of ill will had clearly contributed to the catastrophe.

"This is the first time something like that has happened in my practice," he admitted. Brenner and his team planned to solve the mystery of the Malaysian Boeing as early as 2015. He only added that most likely the stratoliner had landed near the secret Base 211 in Antarctica, which was not such a discovery, but a carefully hidden truth - see - http://www.nzherald.co.nz/mh17-mh370-malaysia-airlines/news/article.cfm?c_id=1503665&objectid=11406800 A new documentary shows how the MH 370 cruise plane flew towards Antarctica. Flight MH 370 may have been hijacked. Of course, someone else was in the cockpit - as this new documentary claims.

Air crash experts analyzed satellite data of the lost Malaysia Airlines flight and found that the plane was still flying for several hours after losing contact with it. Careful examination of the evidence showed that the MH 370 made three turns after the last radio call: first left, then two more - west and then south - toward Antarctica.

According to Malcolm Brenner, the world's leading air crash expert, these turns indicate that someone in the MH 370 cockpit intentionally changed its course.

"This accident caught the world's attention in a way I hadn't seen in forty years in aviation," says Brenner. Claims are filed in a new National Geographic document which will premiere next month, and in which Mr. Brenner and a team of experts try to unravel the mystery of MH 370. "Claims for the MH 370 will be revealed within months, according to the assurances of the Australian search coordinator."

So far it hasn't been found ...

Flight MH 370 disappeared on March 8, 2014 during the flight from Kuala Lumpur to Beijing with 239 people on board. To this day, no traces of the machine have been found, but Mr. Dolan and his team hope to find the wreckage soon.

"I didn't wake up every day thinking, it's going to be that day, but every day I wake up hoping it will, and I expect it to be one day until May," said Commissioner Dolan from News Corp. "It was both incomprehensible and, from our point of view, unprecedented - not only its secrets, but also the scale of the search. So we continue, pointing out that we have not hope but certainty that we will find this missing plane."

Changing the search area for MH 370 is fruitless to this day, as it was believed that the disaster happened in the South China Sea or in the Gulf of Thailand. But then the search area was changed to the southern part of the Indian Ocean.

This is a late operation with no visible signs indicating the wreckage's location, and it is believed that some debris might have appeared off the coast of Sumatra in western Indonesia. Some remains have been found in the Seychelles and Maldives, but it is not certain if they come from this plane.

So far, the searchers haven't had any success and haven't found any plane debris, but experts are trying to predict where the floating models of the plane will end up as it collided with water.

The Search Coordination Center, which is led by Australia, says underwater operations have so far occupied 22,000 square kilometers of the ocean floor, about 36 percent of the exploration priority area. It is believed that if there were no delays with ships, equipment or because of the weather, the underwater search would have in principle been completed in May - and it was already finished with no result ...

The MV Go Phoenix rescue vessel remained in the area, 2,500 kilometers southwest of Perth, Western Australia, but three other vessels involved in the underwater search this week, suspended operations to return to the Australian port for scheduled visits.

During the months of searching, no debris was spotted on the surface of the ocean, nor on the seabed in the area of the search.

25.1. My 2 cents

This information is from two years ago, but there is nothing new in this case. Bloggers from "Base 211" translated the article from the "New Zealand Herald" and supplemented it only with the suggestion that the Malaysian Boeing-777, flight MH 370 flew to Antarctica - to Base 211 in New Swabia, or Queen Maud Land. And it's nice, but it couldn't get there due to lack of fuel. The distance from Kuala Lumpur to the Gulf of Thailand - where the plane made the first turn - then to the northern tip of Sumatra, where the plane turned south for the second time, and to Bowman Island off Wilkes Land in Antarctica, is 8,000 km. And then, flying west to Queen Maud Land, it would have had to travel another 4,000 km - 12,000 km in total without refueling. Assuming it was flying the most straightforward route from Sumatra to Queen Maud Land, it would have had to travel 11,000 km non-stop. Theoretically, it could have reached Antarctica, as the maximum range of the Boeing-777-200 is 14,300 km. But did it really go in this direction? We don't know that.

Besides, the motive. Why would the jet with passengers on board have been hijacked? The key question keeps coming back: what was on board the MH370? Gold? - perhaps. But I'm afraid it was something many times more valuable than gold, namely technologies. They are worth more than the machine and the lives of 239 people. It only remains to answer the questions: Cui bono? Cui prodest? Are the gloomy neo-Nazis of the Andean Fortress behind it?[48]

Robert Leśniakiewicz

---

[48] http://www.base211.ru/?mn=pag&mns=z7tlcd9wnnnq1

Chapter 26

MH370: Norman Davis' Hypothesis and the Moon Landing

Over time, theories and hypotheses have emerged to explain this extraordinary incident, and here they are:

"Crashed MH370 plane found on Google Maps" - such headlines have appeared in the media at least three times recently, arousing the curiosity of those interested in the disappearance of the Malaysia Airlines Boeing 777. The wreckage cannot be found either on computer maps or in reality. And the number of myths surrounding the disappearance of the machine continues to grow.

The official theory, adopted by the Malaysian government and the Australian Transportation Safety Bureau (ATSB), is that in MH370 occured an incident, which left passengers and crew dead of hypoxia. And the plane continued to fly, led by autopilot, until it fell into the ocean.

MH370 went missing on March 8, 2014 on the way from Kuala Lumpur to Beijing. Two hours after take-off, the military radar showed that the machine suddenly left its established route, turned around, and began flying back to Malaysia.

The plane disappeared from radar range and continued the flight for the next 6 hours, during which it contacted the satellites seven times. This contact, known as a handshake, broke off as the plane ran out of fuel. According to data from satellites, the last, seventh, attempt indicated a location in the southern Indian Ocean, near Australia. The eighth attempt to "shake a hand" failed, which means that the plane crashed. Hence the definition of the crash site as "the seventh circle" or "the seventh arc".

What happened at this hour remains a matter of guesswork. The official version says that the first pilot, Zaharie Ahmad Shah, was long unconscious, and because the MH370 ran out of fuel, the plane was flying on autopilot and eventually hit the water. Other theories related to hypoxia include deliberate hijacking (and intentional depressurization of the passenger compartment) or a cockpit fight that would have made the plane to fly steeply upwards, which could have also caused hypoxia, or alternatively some other type of mechanical failure.

Immediately after the disappearance of MH370, former pilot Christopher Goodfellow speculated that there was a fire on board. According to him, this is indicated by the attempt to return to Malaysia, which, according to Goodfellow, could mean looking for an airport for an emergency landing. However, the fire eventually neutralized the pilots, leaving the at least partially flaming plane in the hands of the autopilot.

Patrick Smith, another pilot, questioned the theory regarding the fire on board. He stated that it was unlikely that the MH370 had been able to continue its flight for six hours after the great fire. Officially, the authorities believe that the pilot Zaharie Ahmad Shah was indeed unconscious, but they don't present any theories as to when or why the blackout occurred.

The key point seems to be that the MH370 turned twice: once towards Malaysia and then towards the Indian Ocean. Who made the flight direction change?

History knows quite a few cases of uncontrolled flight after the pilots lost consciousness. Perhaps the most famous is the Helios Airways 522 flight from 2005. 121 people died then after the pilots misinterpreted the alarm signal that was triggered because of decompression in the passenger cabin, and soon lost consciousness themselves due to the progressive climb. The autopilot kept the machine in the air for over an hour before it crashed close to Grammatikos Hill near Athens due to lack of fuel.

That case is so special because one of the people on board probably remained conscious until the end - one of the stewards was using an oxygen cylinder, not a mask, when the pressure in the cabin dropped, and tried to revive the pilots to the end, while calling for help. According to some theories, the same was true for MH370, but it wasn't coincidence.

Some experts believe that the plane was under the control of the captain until the very end, and it was the pilot who consciously brought the machine to the Indian Ocean. Such a theory potentially explains why the plane wasn't found. The search assumed that after running out of fuel, the plane nosed down sharply, hitting the water near the seventh "handshake".

But if Shah was conscious, he could have maneuvered and slowly glided nearly 200 km south. Thanks to this, the plane after hitting the water wouldn't have been badly crashed, nor would there have been a large number of debris, typical of such disasters.

Byron Bailey, a former RAAF coach and Emirates captain as well as one of the proponents of the theory, said that "all indications are" that Shah had hijacked the plane. In 2016, the

Australian Transport Safety Bureau confirmed that Shah's home flight simulator had been used to chart a course to the southern Indian Ocean. Bailey believes that Shah depressurized the plane to neutralize the passengers and crew before he flew south as the only person remaining conscious. "With everyone dead, Zaharie would have pressurized the plane and fly the rest of the trip in comfort," he explained.

In 2016, the then head of the ATSB argued that the pilot-hijacker theory could be considered if the plane's wreckage couldn't be found. But a year later, new data led the Bureau to believe that the plane had been flying out of control at the end. An official report from 2017 concluded that a controlled descent was "very unlikely".

According to another theory, the plane's wreckage is not near Australia, but somewhere north of Malaysia. This theory stems from the method of computing satellite data. As MH370 turned back towards Kuala Lumpur, the last point it was captured by military radar indicated that the plane was traveling slightly northwest, towards India. The problem is that later researchers can rely only on satellite data which doesn't determine the position of the aircraft accurately, but place it within the estimated range in the shape of a circle, with the satellite in the middle.

So it is technically possible that the MH370 was flying inland north instead of south over the ocean. So some speculate that the plane crashed somewhere in central Asia, or was even piloted all the time and safely landed at some hidden airport.

The northern location, however, was ruled out by Inmarsat, the British company that owned and operated the satellite tracking MH370. The company analyzed the data and said it confirms a flight south over the Indian Ocean.

Another point is that if the MH370 were to fly north, it would have traveled for six hours over populated and heavily militarized Central Asian countries such as Kazakhstan and Kyrgyzstan. So it would have been noticed on more than one military radar, and if, for example, it somehow tried to hide from them by flying extremely low, the machine would have been noticed by thousands of people on the way. But no Asian country has confirmed such observations. In 2015, on the beach on the island of Réunion, a two-meter part of the wing (a flaperon), a fragment of an armchair and an airplane window were found. After minor perturbations, it was confirmed that these are the remains of the missing plane. Modeling their drift suggests that they could only end up in this overseas French department if MH370 crashed in the Indian Ocean.

This doesn't convince amateur seekers. Although tens of millions of dollars have already been spent on finding the missing machine, every now and then an internet user claims that, using, for example, Google Maps, it found MH370 crashed (and riddled with bullets!) near Mauritius, in Cambodia, or - as recently - in the Malaysian jungle. You don't have to be a specialist to come up with such a theory, nor do you have to be a specialist to refute it. Most often it is enough to look at previous satellite maps. Then it turns out that the allegedly found machine has been in the place indicated by the Internet user for 10 years (this is the case of Mauritius), or for two months (Malaysia), or it is not a wreck, but a plane flying normally, captured at a given point by a satellite above it.

In June, the final search by RV Ocean Infinity, a private ocean-exploration company, was finished. The search was carried out on a no find, no fee basis, i.e. with payment only when finding the wreckage. Nothing of interest was found. Malaysian authorities have confirmed that there will be no further official searches unless new evidence emerges.

Followers of conspiracy theories don't need it. One of the most interesting, suggested in 2017 by historian Norman Davies, says that after the attacks of September 11, on the on-board computers there was installed a software allowing to take control of the machine in the event of a hijack. Such a computer could have been hacked, reprogrammed, and the intercepted MH370 landed somewhere in Antarctica. In an interview with The Sunday Times, Davies stated that the plane probably had been carrying some secret cargo (or personnel) and had been hijacked ... not once, but twice.

"There have been reports that the cargo details in the on-board manifest don't match. I don't know what the plane might have carried, but it might have been something that someone didn't want to reach China," Davies said. He suggested that there is a possibility that the plane had been hijacked by a hacker and then a second hacker or pilot had taken it over. The first hijack was carried out by the Americans, who wanted the plane not to enter Beijing, and returned it to Diego Garcia (US naval base in the Indian Ocean). Then someone made the second hacking attack and seized the plane so that it wouldn't land in the American base," he said.

In March 2014, a few days after the plane had gone missing, Sunday Express reported that hackers could access the plane's computer via a cell phone and reprogram speed, altitude and direction. After that, it could land or be crashed, the newspaper suggested. It is worth noting that the woman who came to the newspaper with this theory runs her own company that trains businesses and governments to counter terrorist attacks.

Meanwhile, according to Davies, the fate of MH370 can represent a new and terrifying step towards cyberwar, with potentially catastrophic consequences in the future.

Another theory that can't be missed is that the plane was taken over or shot down by the Russians. In fact, Russia was involved in the downing of the Malaysia Airlines Boeing, but not above the Indian Ocean in March 2014, but four months later over the Donetsk region of Ukraine. And it wasn't the MH370, but the MH17 flying from Amsterdam to Kuala Lumpur.

"Russian satellites have seen the wreckage. Putin could have gotten this information," such revelations from the Daily Star were shared by Andre Milne, who previously had appealed for a £1.3m bailout to search for MH370 in the Bay of Bengal. "The reason why President Putin didn't raise his hand and didn't admit finding the wreckage is because he would technically admit to spying," he added.

Another theory is about a mysterious additional passenger who took control of the Boeing 777 and plunged it into the sea. This theory emerged on the day a lawsuit was filed in the US on behalf of the crash victims' families. According to - again - Andre Milne, the plane's official manifesto says 239 people are missing. And in his opinion, there were 226 passengers and 12 crew members on the board, which is a total of 238 people. "An additional passenger could possibly have worked in conjunction with greater external operational support to take full control of the MH370's cockpit," he argued. A spokesman for the investigation team quickly rectified this theory, explaining that the actual number of passengers was 227 and the discrepancy occurs when the manifest is checked two hours before departure. "The actual values may differ from the data sent in the manifest due to last-minute changes," he explained.

New theories are created all the time, even on a regular basis. There are people who have calculated that MH370 has disappeared on the side of the globe opposite to the notorious "Bermuda Triangle" (but probably they haven't paid attention in geography classes), others who say that the missing link in the puzzle is North Korea's participation, or still others who believe in the theory of breaking of vortex energy in a mysterious net of free energy.

Or those claiming that MH370 was skyjacked by Aliens. That's nothing. Three weeks after the plane had gone missing, Sunday Sport announced that the plane was found ... on the moon. The tabloid claims a mysterious flash was observed before the disappearance, the simplest explanation of which is that it was an intergalactic spacecraft that hijacked an entire Boeing 777 and transported it to the moon for some otherworldly reason. If we're to be consistent, the Aliens must have parked the Boeing next to the B-52 bomber that Sunday Sport had found on the moon 26 years earlier. And on Mars it found the statue of Elvis.

However, there are still two theories worth considering. Former Australian Prime Minister Tony Abbott said he believed the MH370 had been intentionally hijacked by a pilot who "had wanted to create the world's greatest secret". "I have always said the most likely scenario is murder-suicide, and if this guy wanted to create the world's greatest mystery, why wouldn't he have fly flown the plane to the end?" he asked on the third anniversary of the plane's disappearance. Investigative journalist Mark Williams-Thomas supports the idea and says the pieces of evidence that have been presented so far point to a deliberate action by the pilot.

According to Williams-Thomas, the wing fragment found on Réunion Island was so far from the search area that it could only appear there if the pilot was intentionally flying to that area. At the same time, he rejects the theory of debris drift, pointing out that there should be a bit more of them, even assuming that the machine settled on the water surface, and didn't crash into it.

The second theory is the idea that the aforementioned MH17 aircraft, shot down over Ukraine, was in fact the MH370. Following this theory, proposed by many sites, including humansarefree.com, MH370 was hijacked and forced to land safely at an undisclosed location. Some point to the previously mentioned American military base on Diego Garcia. Then the plane was deliberately crashed near Donetsk by US agents, a few months later, as part of a false flag operation, i.e. one in which some country operates under the name of another country (e.g. Germans pretending to be Poles, attacking a German radio station on the eve of World War II in Gliwice).

Of course, the operation would have been aimed at discrediting Russia, and the consequences of the catastrophe, according to the followers of this theory, were justified by the reasons. In fact, Russia was accused of providing military support to the Donetsk separatists, including supplying the Buk missile launcher, and the European Union and the US have imposed sanctions on Moscow. On May 24 this year, the international Malaysia Airlines plane crash investigation panel, including representatives from Australia, Belgium, Malaysia, the Netherlands and Ukraine, provided evidence of Russia's role in the 2014 Boeing 777 crash. A day later, the foreign ministers of the Netherlands and Australia accused Russia of being directly involved in the shooting down of the machine. Moscow has consistently denied any involvement in the downing. But it doesn't dispute that it was MH17.

Mass culture often alludes to airplane failures and crashes, from horror films like the 1970 Oscar-winning "Airport" and the recent "Flight" with Danzel Washington, to the famous comedy "Airplane!" The reverse is less common. Meanwhile, after the disappearance of MH370, a theory appeared that, like in the hit series "Lost", the plane crashed in a remote area or even somehow managed to land, and passengers wander somewhere in search of civilization.

Now NBC has produced the series "Manifesto", in which a plane flying from Jamaica to New York falls into turbulence, luckily lands, but it turns out that on its board passed 3 hours, and on the ground - 5 years. "Well, that could explain what happened to MH370" - you can read on many forums.

Another screen adaptations and new theories are a matter of time. Amelia Earhart, whose plane went missing in 1937 during the attempt of a woman's first flight around the world in history, has become the heroine of many films, not only documentaries. In her case, there was also speculation about landing on a desert island, skyjacking by the Japanese or spying for President Franklin Delano Roosevelt.

***

I'm not going to take into account the theories and hypotheses about the fate of the Boeing-777s from the MH-370 and MH-017 flights, because until we find the remains of the former, they are all good for nothing. Idiotic theories about the replacement of planes from flights MH-370 and MH-017 or even more stupid stories about planes on the moon, I send to their place - among fairy tales.

I would like to draw the readers' attention to a significant fact, namely - this is not the first such accident in this region of the world! Working with MSc Stanisław Bednarz over the book on mysterious plane crashes, while composing its statistical part, we noticed that in the area of the Strait of Malacca a few large passenger planes had crashed or disappeared without a trace. So the loss of the Boeing-777 from the MH-370 flight is another such accident!

The second thing. In the film from the series "Expedition to the bottom - Lost plane" broadcast by the National Geographic channel, was shown the search for the wreckage of the MH-370 flight, which led to the finding of the remains of the plane in the western sectors of the Indian Ocean, which indicates that the Boeing 777 fell at 35°S, and from there ocean currents dragged the remains to the beaches of East Africa. And this indicates that the plane was flying until it ran out of fuel and during the eighth hour of flight fell into the ocean, as predicted in the first days of its search.

I'm concerned that the light remains of the Boeing 777 has been "screwed" into the Indian Ocean Gyre and joined the plastic debris floating there. And that's where they should be among the masses of plastics. The rest should lie within the range of the so-called 7th circle, at the bottom of the ocean, around 35°S. Something like this sounds logical.

If the plane became unsealed and people died from lack of oxygen and cold - and all this happened at an altitude of 12,000 m, where the temperature is -50°C - then the plane was guided by an autopilot and fell into the ocean, crashing on its surface. But that was the result of something that had happened a few hours earlier and that for now we don't know.

Perhaps the tragedy of the HA-522 flight in 2005 did repeat there. The depressurization of a cabin at an altitude of 12,000 m can only end in one way ... But we will find out when we have in our hands recorders of flight data and conversations in the cockpit[49].

Robert Leśniakiewicz

[49] https://www.msn.com/pl-pl/wiadomosci/opinie/mh370-hipoteza-normana-davisa-i-lądowanie-na-księżycu/ar-BBOD6b6?ocid=spartanntp&fbclid=IwAR0kq_HvLPlm3Bi2eqC69ixIKnyArrhQy5MwvEd0E7lCxAWXsWLeb1uF0fA#page=1

Chapter 27

Not Only MH-370

My 2 cents regarding flight MH 370. I always try to rationalize any mysterious events and minimize running wild of imagination. For me, the answer is this. The reason was the overlapping of two cases, incorrect flight route programming by the computer and depressurization and autopilot flight until lack of fuel. Here is a list of events with similar circumstances.

On April 20, 1978, an incident with the KAL Boeing 707-321 aircraft took place in the USSR. The plane was flying from Paris to Seoul via Anchorage. The plane passed the checkpoint on

Ellesmere Island in northern Canada, 800 km from the Pole. Here, due to a navigational error, it changed course and flew towards Spitzbergen and the Kola Peninsula in the USSR. After invading the USSR airspace, it was caught up by Su-15 planes. A Soviet pilot identified it as a reconnaissance RC-135. The Air Defense Command ordered it to be shot down. The SU-15 pilot Alexander Bosov informed the headquarters that it was probably a civilian plane. Nevertheless, the command ordered to shoot it down as the plane didn't respond to the calls to follow the fighter and was approaching Finland. The Su-15 pilot fired two missiles, one of them pierced the left wing causing decompression and killing two passengers. After descending from 9000 m, the crew was looking for a place to land for 40 minutes. The plane landed on the frozen lake Korpijarvi in the Karelian ASSR. The landing was successful. Only 2 out of 109 people died. The rest was evacuated and rescued by Soviet helicopters. Initially, they were placed in the town of Kem in a garrison hotel, then the passengers were released at the airport in Murmansk. The crew asked for a pardon and were also released after a procedure lasting several days. The USSR billed Korea for $100,000. There are several doubts as for example, how in 1978, at this level of navigation, it was possible to change the course by 180 degrees and not be aware of it for several thousand kilometers. It was strange downing as only 2 people died. It seems the plane was guided by the fighter to land on the lake.

- On February 13, 1983, Upali Air Learjet 35A disappeared without a trace in Malaysia. The plane was flying from Kuala Lumpur to Colombo. It went missing in the Strait of Malacca 20 km west of Kuala Selangor. The last contact with the plane was 15 minutes after take-off. On February 19, a food kit was found, believed to be from this plane. Ceylon multi-billionaire Upali Wijawardene died. 6 people in total. I would like to add that the Strait of Malacca is as famous there as the Bermuda Triangle ...

- Learjet 25 belonging to Air Traffic Executive Jet airlines, crashed in the Atlantic on 18 May, 560 km NW of Scotland. The plane was flying from Vienna to Hamburg. Contact with it broke 40 minutes after take-off. It hit the Atlantic after running out of fuel. Three people died. The remains have never been found. More details: London, AP, May 19 - West German commercial jet deviated from 1600 mi/~2560 km course on Wednesday, during a training flight from Vienna, and no one from air traffic control could believe it crashed in the Atlantic, 200 mi/320 km south of Iceland.

The US officials in Iceland theorized that the oxygen system had failed, causing the three-man crew to become unconscious. Officials said the pilots probably had died in the crash. The search for the wreckage of the plane was canceled early today.

As the plane flew over northern Europe, British, Dutch and American fighters were sent for interception due to fears that there would be a disaster in a populated area, but the plane flew in a straight line over Scotland and further over the Atlantic at an altitude of about 43,000 ft/~14,330 m.

Two RAF Phantom fighters caught up with it over Scotland, and RAF lieutenant John Marr, the pilot of one of them, said that there was definitely no one in the cockpit. He also thought that there could have been some incident and that the crew might have been lying on board. One theory is that the oxygen delivery system inside the plane broke down and the crew turned on the autopilot, and the pilots left the cockpit to perform an expansion test. Harry Hopkins, a member of the British Flight Safety Committee, said that the biggest secret was the empty space in the cockpit.

"In most emergencies, one pilot is allowed to leave his seat while the other tries to fly a plane," he said. Officials said the Learjet 25B aircraft, owned by the Federal Republic of Germany charter company, departed Vienna on Wednesday at around 3:00 pm CEST for a 450 mi/720 km flight to Hamburg, West Germany. It had fuel for 4 hours of flight. The Learjet 25B has a top cruising speed of almost 550 mph/~ 885 km/h. Manfred Kuppers, Chief Inspector of the Federal Office of West German Aviation in Braunschweig, said radio contact broke off 40 minutes after take-off, when the plane was 12 mi/19 km north of Nuremberg. He said the plane flew over the west of the Netherlands and disappeared from radar screens over the North Sea about 250 mi/400 km northwest of Scotland. Lieutenant Commander William Clyde, spokesman for the US NATO base in Keflavik, Iceland, said the crew was absent and he was fairly certain the oxygen shortage was caused by a malfunction in the aircraft's oxygen delivery system. He also said the plane probably crashed after running out of fuel.

On December 16, 1988, the Learjet 24 belonging to Crown Center Aviation, crashed in Mexico. The plane was flying from Memphis, Tennessee to Dallas, Texas. Two people died, including NASA astronaut Susan Reynolds. The plane continued to fly, passing Dallas. Northrop T-38 Talon fighter was dispatched, but it didn't contact the crew, but only informed that the windows were covered with frost. The plane crashed in Mexico due to lack of fuel, going into a spin near Cuatro Ciénegas, far from Dallas - about 823 km.

- On September 3, 1989, Varig Boeing 737-241 crashed in Brazil. 13 out of 54 people were killed. The plane was flying from Sao Paulo to Belem with several layovers, among others in Maraba. The plane crashed in the jungle during a forced landing 60 km from San Jose. As a result of a mistake, an incorrect route was entered into the on-board computer - instead of the course 0270° (north-north-east), 2700° (west) was typed. After taking off from Maraba, it flew incorrectly to the west and ended up in a remote area in the Amazon rainforest. Attempts to find an alternative airport were unsuccessful. It ended up crash landing on its bottom in the jungle in the dark due to lack of fuel ... It was in the northern part of Mato Grosso on the Xingu River. The survivors were found after two days and taken by helicopter. It was possible due to the fact that, after three hours of hiking in the jungle, healthy people who could walk found a farm. Its residents didn't have a radio, but they went to another farm where people had it. They notified help. The details of the crash have been presented in a film.

-11 September 1990 in the Atlantic Ocean, 290 km from Newfoundland, Boeing 727-247 belonging to the Faucett Perú airlines, flying from Reykjavik in Iceland to Gander in Canada disappeared without a trace. The entire flight was from Malta to Peru. The aircraft, after being leased to Air Malta, returned to Peru in the summer. 16 people went missing: the crew and employees of Faucett. Nobody was found. The plane suddenly disappeared from the radar. The emergency call was heard by the crews of TWA Flight 851 and American Airlines Flight 35. Probably the plane ran out of fuel. Details:

"Faucett's liner was on its way from the Mediterranean island of Malta to Miami with a stopover in Gander, Newfoundland," the Miami director of air operations said. Faucett officials said all 18 people were from Peru, where the airline was based, but one of the crew lived in Miami. Transport

Canada spokeswoman Lily Abbass said the jet had strayed off course and was believed to have plunged Tuesday afternoon approximately 250 mi/400 km SE of St. John's. She said the crew had reported a low fuel level, enough for 30 minute flight, which had its cause in Gander. She said the message was delivered by two American planes. A spokesman for the Coordination Center for Search and Rescue in Halifax said Tuesday evening that a very weak signal from the aircraft's emergency transmitter had been intercepted by satellite after losing radio contact with the crew. However, the CCSR officials said that each time the satellite flew over the body of water, the signal appeared to come from a different location - hundreds of miles away. Rescuers assumed that the plane was in the ocean and sent three Aurora rescue planes and three Labrador helicopters over the water where the signals were last heard. The weather conditions were described as good, and the sea was calm. Several machines flew over the body of water on Tuesday evening, but noticed no one. Two Coast Guard ships, two Fisherman Patrol boats and two destroyers were also sent to the body of water for search. The no longer produced Boeing 727 was designed to be launched and could float for several hours, Boeing spokesman Tom Cole said in an interview in Renton, WA. The plane stopped in Keflavik, Iceland, but the local refueling chief said there were no problems during the stop. Jens Gudmundsson, head of the Reykjavik Air Traffic Control

Center, speculated that "the pilot was lost". "Nobody knows why that plane lost its way," said Betty McDaniel, Faucett spokeswoman in Miami. "This plane has been under an Air Malta contract since May and has been returning to Miami for servicing for the summer months," said Jose Lazaga, the airline's vice president of marketing in Miami. He said there were 18 crew members and family members of company employees on board. "There was one child and four women," said Mrs. McDaniel. Faucett is an airline company based in Lima that handles both cargo and passenger traffic.

- On December 20, 1995, an American Airlines Boeing 757-223 plane crashed in Colombia. 159 people died. The plane, flying from Miami to Cali, hit the El Diluvio mountain (2,700 m above sea level) near the city of Buga. The city of Cali is situated in a narrow valley surrounded by mountains. The plane disappeared from the radar during its landing approach. Then the townspeople heard a roar in the mountains. It turned out that the plane deviated from the route. The difference was 20 km. The teams found 5 alive people on the spot, one of them died in the hospital. It was the most tragic accident involving the Boeing 757. The controllers unnecessarily suggested landing straight from the route, the plane had too high speed for such a landing. Famous passengers include Francisco Ferré Malaussena, Mariana Gómez de Ferré, and Felipe Antonio Ferré Gómez, the son, daughter-in-law, and grandson of the former Miami Mayor Maurice Ferré. Also Paris Kanellakis, a computer scientist at Brown University, died with his wife as well as Maria Teresa Otoya, and the children of Alexander Stephanos. The survivors include Gonzalo Dussan, Monroy Michelle Dussan, Mercedes Ramirez and Mauricio Reyes. Gonzalo "Gonzalito" Dussan Jr., brother of Michelle Dussan and son of Gonzalo Dussan, was initially found alive but died on the operating table due to internal injuries. The crew found a small brown dog that survived in the hold. The dog was taken in by the Red Cross team in Cali, Colombia, and spent there several weeks (they named it Milagro, which means "Miracle" in Spanish). Then an American Airlines employee who worked at the crash site in Cali adopted the dog and brought it to the United States. It is commonly believed that the flight path was incorrectly programmed by the on-board computer.

- On October 24, 1998, Centrafrica Airlines AN-12A crashed in the Democratic Republic of the Congo, then known as Zaire. The plane was flying laden from Goma to Kigali, Rwanda. The plane unexpectedly began to fly to Kisangani in the opposite direction. It crashed near Lubut under unknown circumstances. Three people died. The wreck was found on August 1, 1999. The cause was an incorrectly programmed route.

- On October 25, 1999, the Sunjet Aviation Learjet 35 A crashed in the US. The plane was flying from Orlando, Florida to Dallas, Texas. It crashed in South Dakota near Aberdeen after running out of fuel. The dispatched fighter planes noticed that the windshield was fogged up. All travelers suffocated from lack of oxygen. Six people died, including professional golfer Payne Steward.

- On August 14, 2005, in Greece, the Helios Airways Boeing 737-31 S crashed. 121 people died. The plane flying from Larnaca in Cyprus to Athens and then to Prague crashed as a result of an unfortunate combination of engineers' error during service work and an error of pilots misinterpreting the decompression signal. The service technicians mistakenly switched the oxygen supply mode from automatic to manual. As a result, the oxygen supply stopped working during the climb. An engineer from the tower urged a pilot to make sure that the switch was in the AUTO position. But the pilots suffering from hypoxia couldn't find it. The pilots misinterpreted the distress signal and continued to climb. More and more oxygen was diminishing. People suffocated as did the pilots. The plane remained in the air thanks to the autopilot. After 46 minutes of such a flight around the airport, because the autopilot kept it in this position due to the lack of reaction of the pilots, the plane crashed into the Gramatikos hill near Marathon, 40 km from Athens, despite the attempts of the only conscious flight attendant who had access to an oxygen cylinder. As there was no contact with the plane, two F-16 fighters were sent. They stated that the pilot didn't move, the second seat was empty, and the oxygen masks were hanging ... At the time of the crash, people were suffocated, but alive. Among the victims were 22 children. In addition to 103 Cypriots, there were 12 Greeks. Among the crew was 1 German.

Here are some additional details:

The crash of Boeing-737 belonging to Helios Airways was the greatest disaster in the history of Greek civil aviation. 121 people died in circumstances unknown to this day. The plane, flight number HA522, took off from the airport in Larnaca in Cyprus on August 14, 2005, at 09:00 am EEST. At 10:45 am it should have landed in Athens. At the controls was a German pilot, 58-year-old Hans-Jurgen Merten. The copilot was 51-year-old Pampos Haralambos, who was not inferior to his German colleague both in experience and professionalism. Both recently passed the medical commission examination and both were allowed to fly. Something strange happened during take-off. The pressure in the cockpit and passenger compartment began to drop. Later it turned out that the pilots hadn't turned on the aircraft's air-tight sealing system, although it is always checked three times during pre-flight preparations. At an altitude of 3,600 m, an alarm siren sounded to warn of the danger. Both pilots ignored it. The plane continued its climb. At an altitude of 5,500 m, the emergency safety system was activated. Oxygen masks fell in front of the passengers' faces. The nervous air traffic controllers asked what had happened, but received nonsensical answers. The masks that fell out in the cockpit were ignored: Merten's voice was 5/5 - loud and clear. "Where are the cooling switches?" Merten asked. These were his last words. It was freezing cold in the plane flying slowly up. The oxygen reserve in the masks was calculated for 10-12 minutes. During this time, pilots should have descended to a safe altitude. But Merten and Haralambos had already lost track. The autopilot brought the plane to an altitude of 10,000 m, and the temperature in the passenger cabin dropped to -50°C. The oxygen in the masks ran out. Flight controllers called flight HA522 all the time, but got no response. Planes of the Greek Air Force were raised into the sky. The pilots reported no signs of life on the plane. The pilot's seat was empty, and the copilot lay still on the control panel. Nevertheless, the living man remained on board. Flight attendant Andreas Prodromous took an individual oxygen apparatus, which allowed him to breathe for 10 minutes. Despite the arctic cold, he managed to enter the cockpit and took the pilot's seat. He had a civil aviation pilot's license, but he hadn't learned to fly a Boeing-737. The fighter pilots could only watch helplessly as Andreas tried to control the plane. He was also unable to turn on the radio and establish communication with the flight controller in Athens, and the controller from Larnaca was already out of communication range. After a few minutes, flames came from the port engine - the flight attendant activated something wrong on the control panel. At 12:04 pm the plane lost altitude and crashed near the village of Grammatikos, at the foot of the hill of the same name. The investigation revealed the culprits of this crash - both pilots. They ignored all alarm signals, including the siren and hanging oxygen masks, reason of which remains a mystery to this day. Neither the 1st pilot nor the copilot had reasons to commit suicide. They also couldn't go crazy at the same time. No drugs or alcohol were found in their bodies. The only thing left to suppose was that they had lost their bearings. Maybe we will find the answer to this question someday.

And the biggest hit:

On March 14, 1945, B-17s took off from Italian bases to bomb Komárom on the Danube. A machine from the 301st Bomb Group named Miss BeHaven got damaged over the target. The commander, Lieutenant Walter Podasek, decided to evacuate to the territories occupied by the Russians. When the front line was crossed, the commander - to prevent the plane from going into a spin - activated the autopilot, and the crew parachuted. It happened near Myślenice itself. The most amazing was the finale of this story: the not piloted plane flew over 250 km (!) and made an emergency landing (without landing gear) near Krotoszyn in Greater Poland. Apart from the bent propellers, the machine was undamaged!

Stanisław Bednarz

Chapter 28

The US Navy has the MH-370 search tool, but it's not yet operational...

While the whole world has been interested in what happened to the Malaysian flight MH-370, testers from Edwards AFB in central southern California and Patuxent River NAS in Maryland have worked hard to develop the only tool with which to solve the mystery. Northrop Grumman has built the MQ-4C Triton.

Michael Ballaban has great text describing the U.S. Navy flying combat platforms currently operating in the MH370 search area, including the destroyer and its ASuW and ASW helicopters - the MH-60R (all have since been pulled out for prospecting) and the P-3 Orion and P-8 Poseidon patrol aircraft. They're all good weapon systems, but they're not ideal for finding a metaphorical little bird floating in a huge lake. For what the US Navy considers Broad Area Maritime Surveillance (BAMS), there is no better tool for mankind to search than the MQ-4C Triton, which is under development.

The program of the new American spy drone finally went into effect. The ocean is huge, it would be easy for a whole fleet of surface ships to hide in it, if not ...

Based on an enlarged version of the Northrop Grumman (UAS) semi-autonomous unmanned aerial vehicle system. This High Altitude Long Endurance (HALE) drone has the ability to fly for over 24 hours at speed of up to 330 kts/611 km/h. It can explore a massive 2,700,000 square miles/69,900,000 km² of sea or shoreline in one flight. It can scan 2,000 square miles with a single radar move, and it can do it virtually in any direction, in a two-dimensional plane. The aircraft's ability to survey such large areas of the planet simultaneously is a result of its operating altitude of nearly 55,000 ft/16,667 m and its incredibly powerful and versatile rotating radar system.

The Triton AN/ZPY-3 MFAS is an active, electronically scanning, 360-degree X-band radar. It has been specially designed for maritime surveillance, but can also sniff from shore and land lines. The unique ability of this radar to see in all directions around the aircraft, at great distances, while accurately focusing on one point of the sea or the shoreline, gives the MQ-4C the possibility not only to detect surface targets over long distances, but also track them. By using MFAS in reverse synthetic aperture mode (in which the radar takes a map-like image), Triton can shoot a very focused beam of powerful radar energy at a small target hundreds of miles away and "see" what that target is. The system can also quickly scan large areas of the sea and instantly take high-resolution radar pictures only of contacts (ships) it receives during such a scan. Triton can then efficiently classify and/or identify these targets using advanced image recognition and radar software, and read ship transponders with an on-board Automatic Identification System (AIS). In this way, analysts at the Triton ground control station, which can be located in different parts of the world, can immediately see not only the location of all targets Triton has detected, but also radar images with the synthetic aperture of these targets. Moreover, since Triton can classify the targets it detects itself, the operator can select filters so that Triton only transmits the target images that the operator instructs the system to send, thus saving bandwidth, time and manpower.

Triton's ability to "distill" most of the data it receives, while leaving operators a look at only the most relevant information it collects, fits well with Global Hawk's "semi-autonomous" command and control concept. The concept is that "flying" the drone is done by pointing and clicking on a location on the map and setting the speed, altitude and target of the aircraft using the dashboard interface. The idea is to automate as many functions as possible, thereby increasing the productivity of the workforce while reducing the time it takes to use significant intelligence.

When an image of the radar with synthetic aperture that is sensitive to weather conditions just doesn't provide information, the massive Triton, which has a wingspan like that of a Boeing-757, can do what its Global Hawk cousins can't do, go down to a low level to explore the target up close and personally.

Triton has been designed with a much more durable fuselage that is more resistant to hail, birds and lightning strikes, compared to the RQ-4B Air Force, and also includes anti-icing systems on the wings. These features allow it to descend to lower altitudes in unfavorable weather conditions, to get a closer look at the target thanks to the Raytheon multispectral electro-optical/infrared sensor built into the MTS-B spectrometer. This highly efficient senor sphere has been used for some time on the MQ-9 Reaper unmanned aerial vehicle, and in its latest form it offers a wide range of infrared sensitivity as well as standard electro-optical visualization. In addition, the MTS-B can be equipped to provide laser marking, pointer and range determination capability. This sensor, connected to the Triton powerful mission computers, can also track automatically as well as be subordinated, to independently search for any contact detected by the Triton powerful MFAS radar.

The Triton advanced optical package will not only allow it to send photos of the target in question from a distance and at close range, but it will also be able to set targets and provide live view during special missions. This ability to explore a target to the last mile, literally from detecting a suspicious radar track hundreds of miles away, to reading a name painted on the side of a ship, is truly stunning and fills the conceptual "tactical" gap that traditionally existed in the case of such large, wide-scanning, strategic surveillance resources.

Triton is also hell for the passive listener. The aircraft will be equipped with a modular Electronic Support Measures (ESM) kit, which was borrowed from the EP-3 Aeries spy plane. This system can smell radar signals, even faint ones, and classify them. Furthermore, such a system should also be capable of triangulating and geolocating these signals. This data can be used for strategic purposes by planners who build an enemy profile in the form of an "electronic battlefield", or it can be used to keep Triton, and even the other planes it transmits (more on that in a moment), out of the enemy radar range and the capabilities of ground missiles. The system can also be used to locate ships at sea as most of them use at least one type of radar for navigation, while larger military units usually have many types of powerful radar systems that are easily detectable over long distances. In this sense, the ESM Triton could be just as useful for detecting surface vessels through its advanced radar system.

While such a system focuses on detecting radar emissions, as Triton grows, it should be able to monitor other signals, and eventually also provide communications surveillance as well as be capable of listening for various types of telecommunications means. All this means that Triton will be just as good as a passive detection platform and will be able to track with fantastic accuracy certain radar or communication emissions coming from the silently electromagnetic ocean.

Finally, the MQ-4C has the ability to act as a network relay and data fusion center. In other words, it can act as a mainframe flying server and set of antennas, transmitting and receiving messages from the entire theater of warfare, between weapons systems and/or commanders that are not in sight. The MQ-4C can also receive what ships, planes and land sensors see and transmit via various data link systems around the battlefield, and combine this information into a common "picture". It can then resend that enhanced image back to the same platforms and/or commanders around the world. This capability provides a vastly improved "active network" on the maritime battlefield, and drastically enhances the interoperability, situational awareness, aiming performance and image clarity of sensors for all forces while providing a resilient alternative to sensitive satellite communications systems.

So when you have to look for something in the water but have no idea where it is in the better half of the hemisphere, the best way to find it is to release Tritons. They can scan a larger area in a single segment than any other platform in the world, and are able to independently examine each interesting contact using optical or infrared radar and its advanced capabilities of listening intelligent signals, and if needed, they can go low and stream live video to the command and control module. Additionally, Triton can help coordinate searches with other platforms by sharing target data and sending messages far beyond the horizon. Interoperability with the new P-8 Poseidon, which is making its international debut in the search for the MH-370, was part of the original objectives of the Triton mission, and together they form one dream team exploring the surface and area below the sea.

Once the MQ-4C becomes operational, which should be within a few years, we will look back at the archaic search for the MH-370 as the last mass use of enormous manpower in an international sea search of this kind. In the future, when such a sad event happens and the US Navy orders the search for the proverbial needle in a bottle of hay, although of water, the question will be: "Where are Tritons?"[50]

Tyler Rogoway

---

[50] Jalopnik - https://foxtrotalpha.jalopnik

Chapter 29

Flight MH370: series of control failures?

Air traffic control failure series. Air traffic controllers lost the MH370 plane during a crucial 18-minute timeslot, meaning the mystery of the missing plane could never be solved...

29.1. MH370 - what happened?

Malaysia Airlines flight MH370 took off from Kuala Lampur and headed for Beijing with 239 people on board. Among the passengers were Chinese calligraphers, a couple traveling home to their sons after a long-delayed honeymoon, and a construction worker who hadn't been home in a year. But at 00:14 am MYT on March 8, 2014, Malaysia Airlines lost contact with the Boeing-777 near Phuket Island in the Strait of Malacca. Before that, the Malay authorities had heard the last words coming from the plane, either said by the captain or by the copilot, and they were: "Goodnight Malaysian three seven zero." Satellite 'pings' from the plane suggest that it continued flight for about seven hours until it ran out of fuel. Experts have calculated that it had fallen approximately 1,000 mi/~1,600 km west of Perth, Australia. But the great search by the services and the military at the bottom of the ocean was unsuccessful. The wreckage wasn't found and a whole bunch of alternative theories about its fate emerged.

Air traffic controllers lost the cursed flight MH370 during the crucial 18-minute timeslot, raising concerns that the mystery would never be resolved. The packed passenger jet disappeared from the air traffic control radar screens in Malaysia, 5 seconds after it had entered Vietnam's airspace.

But the controllers monitoring the flight in Kuala Lumpur were busy with other flights and simply didn't notice that it had disappeared. The inspector said that when he had realized it, he had assumed the machine had been in the hands of his Ho Chi Minh counterparts. However, Vietnamese controllers saw the Boeing 777 - which disappeared with 239 people on board - entering their airspace and then disappearing.

After that, they apparently misunderstood the rules, which meant they should have informed Malaysia immediately if the plane didn't show up.

Some believe that the plane obviously turned shortly after entering Vietnamese airspace. The controllers repeatedly tried to contact the plane - which is believed to have crashed in the ocean - but to no avail. 18 minutes had passed since its sudden disappearance by the time they finally informed Kuala Lumpur by phone.

"There was an operation full of 'confusion and incompetence' mistakes," say those close to the lengthy investigation.

They say the Kuala Lumpur Air Rescue Coordination Center should have been notified within an hour of the disappearance. But it took over four hours to inform the rescuers - making it virtually impossible to pinpoint where and when it fell.

Five fragments, possibly from the Malaysia Airlines plane, were later washed ashore on Madagascar - more than 4,500 miles from Vietnam.

Aviation expert Victor Iannello believes that one piece, which appears to be a part of the inner floorboard, has been damaged by a "high velocity impact".

Over the past five years, more than 30 pieces of aircraft have been collected from around the world. However, only three wing fragments that has been washed ashore by the Indian Ocean are confirmed to be from the missing flight.

Earlier this year, it was reported that the pilot "had controlled the machine to the end" but had made "unusual" turns before crashing. French investigators were granted access to a "significant amount" of flight data transmitted during the flight before the crash. Official documents say that the pilot Zaharie Ahmad Shah (53) crashed the plane into the ocean thereby committing suicide.

It is said that the doomed plane was mysteriously "circling" and "turning" shortly before disappearing. Data from British satellites may indicate that the Boeing 777 was strangely wheeling over the Pacific Ocean in Southeast Asia at the time it disappeared.

Aviation expert Jeff Wise, author of The Plane That Wasn't There, said that Inmarsat data could suggest that the MH370 had been flying strangely in its final minutes. Normally, a jet circles at a fixed altitude after it receives an instruction from the air traffic control before being cleared to land at the airport.

A satellite called 3F1 made contact with the plane hours after it had gone missing, by a series of technically so-called electronic "handshakes".

Wise explained:

"Just as the movement of a speeding train causes its whistle tone to rise or fall, the relative movement of the satellite and the plane alters the frequency of the radio signals transmitted between them."

The disappearance of MH370 has also sparked a plethora of conspiracy theories - some far more weird than others.

***

29.2. Here are some theories about MH370 flight:

• Vladimir Putin - some blame Russian President Vladimir Putin for being involved in the hijacking of flight MH370. American science writer Jeff Wise accused Putin of "confusing" the navigation of the plane by sending false data to the crew (via GLONASS???), which caused the plane to fly undetected to the Baikonur spaceport, Kazakhstan, in order to "Harm the West."

• The Americans shot down the plane. Former Air France director Marc Dugain accused US military of shooting down the plane due to the fear it had been hijacked. (The plane could have been used as a missile - as was the case in New York on September 11, 2001 - against the airbase on Diego Garcia in the Indian Ocean.) In the book Flight MH370 - The Mystery he also suggests that the aircraft could have been shot down incidentally by US and Thai fighters during military exercises, and the evidence classified.

• Suicide - Malaysian police chief Gen. Tan Sri Khalid Abu Bakar has suggested that the disappearance was a result of committing suicide. He claimed that someone on board might have bought a large life insurance package before the flight to provide its family a treatment or pay off the money owed.

• In hiding? Historian and writer Norman Davies has suggested that the MH370 may have been hacked remotely and thus skyjacked to some secret location to seize some valuable cargo that was aboard.

• Slots in the plane? Malaysia Airlines found a 15-inch/~38.1 cm gap in the fuselage of one of their planes, days before the disappearance of MH370. The FAA insisted on issuing a final warning two days before the disappearance of the Boeing 777. But the Daily Mirror claimed the missing jet "hadn't have the same antenna as the rest of the Boeing 777s," so it hadn't received the warning.

• The pilot planned the disaster - Prime Minister Malcolm Turnbull unexpectedly said that it was very possible that it was the pilot who had planned this shocking event. He accused the pilot of wanting to create the world's greatest secret. Another theory claims that the pilot hijacked the plane in protest of the arrest of Malay opposition Anwar Ibrahim, who wanted to destabilize the corrupt government of Najib Razak. Another version of this theory is that the pilot deliberately wrecked the plane, but before parachuted out and then spent the rest of his life with a lover who waited for him in a boat at sea.

• North Korea hijacked the plane. In the chronicles of the incidents, South Korea recorded a case in which North Koreans hijacked a Chinese plane with 220 passengers on board on March 5, 2014. Some in Pyongyang wanted to shoot down the plane, but others wanted to hijack it and deliver it to North Korea to convert the travelers to communism.

• Victims' cell phones rang ... One theory claims that since many relatives were able to hear the ringing for up to four days after the crash, the jet couldn't crash into the Indian Ocean. Nineteen families said their loved ones' devices rang up to four days after the jet went missing, but wireless analysts say telephone companies sometimes use phantom signal when the device is inactive, reports the Daily Star. (The thing is, the Daily Star is the same colored tabloid as the Daily Mail or The Sun, and therefore rather unreliable ...)

• It crashed in the Cambodian jungle. In September 2018, British video producer Ian Wilson claimed to have found a missing plane using Google Maps. Although millions have been spent searching for the wreckage, British investigators believe they found the plane in the mountainous area of the Cambodian jungle. In response, the Chinese government used the Space View observation company to focus on a high-altitude area on the outskirts of Phnom Penh, but the company found no trace of any aircraft. One MH370 specialist claimed that locals in Cambodia told him that they had seen in a jungle a plane believed to have been the Malaysia Airlines plane.

• The plane was flying to Kazakhstan. If the jet was going north, the possible locations could extend as wide as the border between Kazakhstan and Turkmenistan, all the way to Thailand. Malaysia's Prime Minister Najib Razak initially asked the Kazakh leader Nursultan Nazarbayev to start a search operation in the country, but soon after he withdrew his request when rescue efforts focused on the Indian Ocean.[51]

Jon Lockett

---

[51] „The Sun" - https://www.thesun.co.uk/news/10537002/mh370-air-traffic-controllers-mystery-never-solved

Chapter 30

Poison Tea?

Disappearance of the flight MH370. Shocking explanation

Malaysia Airlines plane (flight MH370) went missing on March 8, 2014. There were 239 people on board. No bodies or wreckage have ever been found. Experts believe it was a skyjacking and the passengers were given tea to get numb.

According to the latest reports, the missing plane was hijacked and the passengers were given a sedative so that they wouldn't interfere with the activities. The theory was developed by Egyptian aviation expert Ismail Hammad, who presented what the last moments on board could look like.

What happened to the flight MH370 from Kuala Lumpur to Beijing remains unknown. The plane took off on March 8, 2014 around 00:40 am MYT. It last contacted the control tower 40 minutes later, at 01:19 am. It strayed from the track and was in the air for another 7 hours without responding to any call. It probably crashed between 08:19 and 09:15 am.

There were 239 people on board, including 12 crew members. So far, no plane wreckage, no black boxes or the bodies of passengers have been found. Over the years, many theories have emerged as to what could have caused the catastrophe.

According to the latest theory, the plane was hijacked. During the investigation it turned out that two or three passengers had possessed false European passports and that they presumably had taken control of the flight. They were probably of Iranian origin and wanted to travel to Europe to obtain asylum.

According to Ismail Hammand, for them to hijack the plane, they would have needed to be in control of the passengers. They could give them a special tea that was supposed to make them so numb that they didn't protest. It could also be poison - there are theories that everyone on board was dead at the time of the crash.

I have no doubts that what happened, affected everyone on board. The hijacker had to screen passengers and security personnel as part of his swift action, Hammand told the Daily Star.

The Egyptian expert also added that the hijackers planned to land on one of the islands in the Philippines. The airports there are not adapted to landing of large passenger planes and their lanes are too short. The machine might not have aimed and crashed into the sea.[52]

---

[52] https://www.o2.pl/artykul/samolot-zaginal-z-239-pasazerami-po-latach-zagadka-sie-wyjasnia-6467272075486849a

30.1. My 2 cents

The theory as good as any other. Perhaps the passengers and crew were drugged and the plane was seized. Question: how did it look technically? How were nearly 250 people made to drink poisoned tea? Personally, I think that the best effect would have been to depressurize the plane at the cruising altitude - almost 12,000 m.

Hijacking a plane from Kuala Lumpur to fly to Europe? It doesn't make sense, considering that the plane COULDN'T do this with full fuel tanks, and being undetected. Besides - assuming they could do it - they realized they would have had to serve a sentence for skyjacking. Of course, being a prisoner in Iran, and in Europe are two different things, but still they would have been 10-20 years behind. And that's not what they wanted ...

Landing in the Philippines? Perhaps, but given the population density of 357.2 people/km², someone would simply have to had seen it! So an incredible story ...

Aldona Brauła

Chapter 31

Ghost Plane: Flight MH-370 - Anatomy of the Crash

Finally, an excellent and detailed summary of this remarkable case by Dr. Miloš Jesenský, and here it is:

31.1 Without a trace

One of the first pieces of information that circulated in the world media on March 8, 2014 was the ominous news that

Malaysia Airlines Boeing-777 had disappeared during a scheduled flight from Kuala Lumpur to Beijing. Television viewers, readers of reputable websites or the daily press didn't learn anything more than that air traffic controllers lost contact with the Boeing after about two hours, when it was flying in good weather over the South China Sea. Vietnamese media reported that the machine crashed without sending a signal for help, while Malay Communications Minister Hishamuddin Hussein only spoke of lossing communication with the crew.

Let's try to get the starting facts: The Boeing 777-200 took off from Sepang Airport in Kuala Lumpur on Saturday at 00:21 am MYT and was due to land in Beijing at 06:30 am CST with 227 passengers on board. However, it didn't.

The news portal "The Star"[53] wrote, among other things, that the plane had had fuel in its tanks for 7 hours of flight, so it was supposed to stay in the air until 08:30 am. This clearly shows that it may have landed somewhere outside the flight route or have crashed. The site where this tragedy was to take place was located by the Vietnamese emergency services who went there. Unfortunately, no remains were found anywhere on the flight route and the pilot didn't send a call for help, which was

---

[53] „Flight MH370 bound for Beijing goes missing" -
https://www.thestar.com.my/News/Nation/2014/03/08/Missing-plane-MAS/

unusual in itself. However, a similar incident happened in 2009, when an Air France plane flying from Brazil to France fell into the Atlantic waves without any call for help.

The search in the South China Sea was further complicated by territorial disputes between China and the Philippines in this basin. In spite of this, the Chinese sent two rescue ships there, and the Filipinos sent three patrol boats and three reconnaissance planes.

"In such situations, we must act together, without regard to border problems," said General Roy Deveraturd, commander of the Philippine Western Military District.

On the very first day of the search, the pilots of Vietnamese planes found a large stain of oil on the sea surface.

"A Vietnamese navy plane discovered an oil stain about 20 km in length in the area where the disaster might have occurred. We suspect that it is related to the missing Boeing. We didn't announce this find, but we are still searching," the New York Times[54] quoted the statement of the director of the Vietnamese Civil Aviation Authority - Laj Suan Than. Meanwhile, Malaysian Insider, citing Chinese sources, wrote

---

[54] FULLER, Thomas – SCHMITT, Eric: „Passport Theft Adds to Mystery of Missing Malaysia Airlines Jet" -
https://www.nytimes.com/2014/03/09/world/asia/malaysia-airlines-flight.html?hp&_r=0

that the plane had never entered China's airspace, and the air traffic control had seen the plane approximately halfway between Malaysia and Vietnam, at an altitude of 10.6 km.

By that time it was clear that a disaster must have occurred, when the information that the wanted Boeing had to make an emergency landing in the South China city of Nan-ning and that its signal was picked up 220 km from the South Vietnamese province of Ca Mau, wasn't confirmed. On the afternoon of March 8, was published a list of people traveling on this plane, among which were also 5 young children. Although the crew was entirely Malay, the passengers were mostly Chinese - 152 people. There were also Malaysians - 38, Indonesians - 7, Australians - 6, Indians - 5, French - 4 and 3 Americans. Apart from them, there were citizens of: New Zealand, Ukraine, Canada, Russia, Italy, Taiwan, the Netherlands and Austria.

On March 9, 2014, the pilots of one of the 22 search aircraft conducting the search along with 40 ships and naval craft noticed objects on the sea surface that could belong to the missing Boeing-777. One Reuters[55] whistleblower interested in

---

[55] GOVINDASAMY, Siva: „Exclusive: Malaysia plane probe narrows on mid-air disintegration – source". - https://www.reuters.com/article/us-exclusive-probe-plane/exclusive-malaysia-plane-probe-narrows-on-mid-air-disintegration-source-idUSBREA280FF20140309

the search said the plane may have disintegrated at the altitude of 10,000 meters, which could explain why no debris was found, and no signals were received from the black boxes of the missing plane. Meanwhile, "The Star"[56] reminded that the same was the case with the search for the French Airbus A-330 in 2009, when rescuers had found dead bodies and the remains of the machine on the surface of the ocean for several weeks, and the wreckage and black boxes were lifted from the seabed after two years. The conclusion is that if the plane fell into the sea in one piece, many debris would float on the surface, and if the plane fell apart as a result of a mechanical failure or explosion at high altitude, the bodies and luggage of travelers would be scattered over a large area.

31.2. Mysterious passengers on board

The list of passengers and missing persons included an Italian and an Austrian, but neither Luigi Maraldi nor Christian Kozel has gotten a hair of his head harmed to this

---

[56] „Confounding mystery of the missing airliner Flight did not send distress call after final point" -
https://www.thestar.com.my/News/Nation/2014/03/09/Confounding-mystery-of-the-missing-airliner-Flight-did-not-send-distress-call-after-final-point-of/

day. How is it possible? It's very simple - their documents were previously in the hands of Asian thieves. Thus, among the passengers there had to be two people with a false identity. Therefore the services dealt with the hypothesis of a terrorist attack in combination with other forms of organized crime, such as illicit arms trafficking and drug smuggling.

As reported by the Italian daily La Repubblica, 37-year-old Luigi Maraldi is doing well, he is in Thailand, and in early August 2013 he reported the theft of his passport to the authorities. As soon as Malaysia Airlines released the passenger list, Italian TVs immediately launched a search. The police soon after entered Maraldi's house to inform his old parents about the sad event. However, when they knocked on the door, they found the old couple calm, because literally a moment earlier their son called from Thailand that he was fine. What is paradoxical is that his parents didn't know anything about this misfortune because they didn't watch any news service that day.

In 2012, 30-year-old Christian Kozel also lost his document, which was confirmed by the spokesman of the Austrian Ministry of Foreign Affairs to the reporters of Die Welt[57]. But who was flying with his passport, we don't know ... The media

---

[57] HEGMANN Gerhard: „Mindestens zwei Unbekannte an Bord der Boeing 777", -
https://www.welt.de/vermischtes/article125581200/Mindestens-zwei-Unbekannte-an-Bord-der-Boeing-777.html

began to incline to the hypothesis that the cause of the plane's disappearance could be a terrorist attack.

But let's return to the false identities of both travelers. Reporters from the American television network CNN[58] discovered that tickets for both stolen passports had been purchased by unidentified men through the Chinese company China Southern Airlines website. The boarding pass numbers were successive, ergo the airlines issued them at the same time. In Kuala Lumpur, two men boarded a plane to Beijing, from where they were to fly to Amsterdam. They were supposed to split up there - the passenger with the stolen Italian passport was to go to Copenhagen, and the passenger with the Austrian one - to Frankfurt. Investigators therefore began to examine the recordings of camera monitoring from the departure hall of the Malaysian metropolis. In addition to the identity of the people boarding the plane, they were also interested in the course of security checks, during which there was a clear breach of official regulations - no one with a false or not their passport should have been allowed to board the plane. This situation was referred to by the then director of Interpol, Ronald Noble, who criticized the insufficient attention of the authorities:

---

[58] HILLS, Mike: „Mystery of flight MH370 raises fears of passport fraud" dostępne na https://www.bbc.com/news/world-asia-26531175

"While it is too early for us to link these two stolen passports with the disappearance of the plane, it raises serious concerns that some passenger could board the plane for an international flight, based on a stolen document that is in our police databases.[59]" Even though the theft of these documents had been reported long before, the officials who were to check them, didn't use the international database.

According to CNN[60], the tickets were purchased by a man of Iranian origin, and the British daily The Guardian[61] claims that investigators are checking the identities of four travelers.

Thai authorities carried out over a dozen police raids on secret false passport factories on the island of Phuket. Malaysian police managed to quickly identify one of the passengers of flight MH-370, who was traveling with a stolen passport. Investigator Khalid Abu Bakar announced that it was

---

[59] PEARSNON, Michael – SAAAED, Ahmed: „Who were the mystery men on missing Malaysia Airlines Flight 370?" -
https://edition.cnn.com/2014/03/10/world/asia/malaysia-airlines-mystery-passengers/index.html

[60] BRANIGAN, Tanja: „Malaysia Airlines: identities of four passengers being investigated" -
https://www.theguardian.com/world/2014/mar/09/malaysia-airlines-missing-plane-fears-worst

[61] HETTER, Katia – CRIPPS, Karla: „Who travels with a stolen passport?" - https://edition.cnn.com/2014/03/10/travel/malaysia-airlines-stolen-passports/index.html

a 19-year-old Iranian who had wanted to emigrate to Germany and most likely hadn't been a member of any terrorist group. However, in this case, the word "most likely" must be treated with considerable reserve ...

31.3. Following traces of the stolen passports

The mystery of the missing flight MH-370 poses a cardinal question: is it possible to board the plane with a false or stolen passport? According to CNN reporters[62], it's not that complicated. However, how is this possible, when most of us have experienced this complicated check-in at international airports - removing shoes, belts, leaving bottles filled with mineral water, careful luggage inspection, x-raying and checking of identity and travel documents?

It is feasible because a passport can be checked several times before boarding, but as long as it is not compared with Interpol's lost document database, a passenger using a false document can go through all the checks without problems.[63]

---

[62] MATURA, Jan: „Letadlo duchů si to štrádovalo po Asii jako o nedělní vycházce" - https://www.idnes.cz/technet/technika/zmizeni-boeing-777-200er-malaysia-airlines-mh370.A140316_221604_tec_technika_jm

[63] Most European border services have their own lost documents

This sounds very alarming, because it leads to the conclusion that 1/3 of passengers can get on board with a false passport[64]. According to the International Air Transport Association, so far over 3.1 billion travelers have been transported by planes, of which over 1 billion didn't have their passports compared with the Interpol database! And this is where the rhetorical question is raised, why only a handful of countries make sure that people with stolen or forged passports don't get on board aircraft on international or intercontinental flights, for only the United States alone records 300,000 lost or stolen documents??? The number of queries to the Interpol database per year varies around 800,000, of which 60,000 are positive results.

In Poland, Slovakia and the Czech Republic, all passports and other identity documents are checked for flights in the airspace of the Schengen countries, therefore it is difficult to understand a different approach on a European scale. However, we must be aware that a large part of the 190 Interpol countries does not always and everywhere have the technical capacity and resources to ensure permanent access to the database.

"I sincerely hope all governments and airlines will learn from the tragedy of the lost flight MH370 and begin routinely

dossier, which they use during passport and customs clearance.

[64] Rather with not his own passport, or with a modified or forged one.

checking all passports before allowing passengers to board the plane," said Interpol Secretary Ronald Noble.

Unfortunately, to this day many have not taken his statement to heart.

31.4. Before disappearing: explosion, fight or collapse?

"It seems unbelievable that a large communication plane will change course, fly somewhere over Asia, and then disappear without a trace," Czech journalist Jan Matura writes in the margin of the lost flight MH-370. "At a time when anyone can read your SMS and in the sky we are followed by unmanned drones, the layman must think that in the case of the missing Malaysian Boeing, someone was pulling the strings."[65]

And yet it is true that this event is even darker than at the time of its inception, because even six years after the incident, we are not able to answer the question of what happened to the "ghost plane" and the unfortunate passengers on board.

---

[65] „Was Missing Plane's Transponder Turned Off?" -
https://news.sky.com/story/was-missing-planes-transponder-turned-off-10413823

Let's ask ourselves, how is it possible that such a large plane as the Boeing-777 could completely disappear from the radar? There is no simple answer to this when we introduce ourselves to the enormous number of instruments on the plane, including UHF and VHF radio stations, automatic transmitters, GPS and computer communication systems. On the other side of the multi-unknown equation, trajectory data is missing, and the search area contains a huge body of water and sparsely inhabited lands of jungle and mountains.

But how do you explain that the pilots didn't send the Mayday signal, or even the Pan-pan? The explanation would be the situation of immediate disintegration of the machine - e.g. in the event of an explosion on board, shooting down or disintegration of the plane due to a technical failure. There were also speculations that the plane, or rather its electronics, was hacked with the use of an electronic entertainment system for travelers. It is equipped with USB ports for transferring multimedia resources, and with some skill in manipulating it, it would be possible to master the electronic infrastructure of the machine and its safety, service and control systems.

The interesting thing is that for some reason the plane's transponder, or the cockpit radio, which cooperates with the ground-based radar when it receives its signal and responds with a code with the aircraft's position, flight altitude and call signal, stopped working. Flight controllers use its signals to determine the speed and direction of flight of an airplane. Why the transponder went silent is one of the basic, cardinal questions. Such device is placed between two pilots and can be turned off very easily. According to an experienced pilot Mark Weiss, switching off is very unlikely, because this device provides very important information to the crew and cannot be turned off for flight safety reasons. Without black boxes, and therefore without a record of the cockpit conversations and the logbook, it will be very difficult to find out what happened in the cockpit, Weiss says. Other experts differ in views on the deliberate deactivation of the transponder. According to some, it was turned off by, for example, a hijacker, according to others, the electrical system supplying the transponder could fail.[66]

If there was a hijacking and its perpetrators wanted to make the plane "invisible" by turning off all instruments and the transponder - the plane would have not disappeared from the radar screens, because its fuselage would have still reflected the radar waves. So, if the crew were forced to turn off the devices, the plane would have only disappeared from one type of radar. On another, which shows the image of the plane as a real,

---

[66] MIDDLETON, Jason: „What could have happened to flight MH370?" - http://theconversation.com/what-could-have-happened-to-flight-mh370-24161

physical object, it would have been constantly visible, which, however, depends on the radar coverage of the area, the type of radar, and the rotational speed of the antenna per minute. A radar operating in the 1 m band can - under normal conditions - detect and observe planes at a distance of 850-1000 km, while in the lower bands with a higher frequency this distance is reduced.

However, if there was a terrorist attack and an immediate interruption of communications, it had to be carefully planned, as Jason Middleton, dean of the Department of Aeronautics at the University of New South Wales, claims on The Conversation. In his opinion, an explosive charge could have exploded in the space behind the cockpit, causing great damage. Another possibilities are the deliberate detonation of a bomb in the front part of the plane - e.g. in toilets, or an attack on the pilots in the cockpit, which terrorists somehow entered. Such a surprise attack on the crew would explain why the pilots didn't transmit the Mayday or Pan-pan signal and the four-digit code: 7500 (hijack) or 7700 (threat).

In clarifying this puzzle, it would be of great help to check the contents of the black boxes, the radio transmitters of which are calibrated in such a way that when the g-force exceeds 8 g[67],

[67] 1 g is the value of the gravitanional acceleration - where 1 g = 9.81 m/s^2.

they activate automatically. Their radio signals can then be picked up by special devices from the decks of ships or naval craft. When submerged in water, these devices emit an ultrasonic signal at a frequency of 37.5 kHz for one month after activation. The missing Boeing, however, belonged to the older generation of these machines, which were equipped with the fourth generation black boxes. Nevertheless, they provide at least one-way data telemetry (from board to ground station), and data is stored in a multi-track recording in two independent devices of the airplane. Concurrently, they broadcast it directly or by satellite to the Boeing Air Operations Center in real time.[68]

In connection with a possible technical failure, there were also comments related to the report of a harmless collision between Malaysia Airlines Boeing 777-200 and Airbus A-340 belonging to China Eastern Airlines two years earlier. During taxiing at Pudong Airport, the two machines rubbed against each other, and the Boeing lost part of its wing. Fortunately, no one was hurt and the planes were put into service after repairs.[69]

---

[68] Boeing Commercial Services -
http://www.boeing.com/commercial/services/

[69] PARRIE, Lizzie: „Missing Malaysia Airlines Boeing 777 feared crashed off Vietnam 'collided with another plane breaking its wingtip two years ago" - https://www.dailymail.co.uk/news/article-2576353/Malaysian-Airlines-Boeing-777-centre-crash-probe-

Both the airline and the aircraft manufacturer have detailed technical data on the condition of their aircraft before its disappearance, which makes it possible to judge whether there could have been a malfunction, temperature increase, fuel leakage, and so on, and so forth. However, from this information attack by terrorists or skyjackers cannot be deduced. CVR, or Cockpit Voice Recorder, is located in boxes on board the plane. In addition, the next generation of black boxes will automatically send a coded signal to Malaysia Airlines' Air Operations Center in the event of an on-board explosion or downing.

31.5. Conversations with ghosts

On March 11, 2014, sensational information began to spread around the world that some relatives called the cells of their missing family members, stating that the phones were still working, but no one was answering the calls[70]. Others claimed

---

collided-plane-two-years-ago-breaking-wingtip.html

[70] „Smartphones of missing aboard flight MH370 'are still ringing', families say." - https://www.dailymail.co.uk/news/article-2578020/Why-cellphones-missing-Malaysian-Airlines-passengers-

that their phone numbers were still active in China's QQQ cellular network, which would mean their status was still online. These attempts again caused a wave of hope and frustration - according to them the phones of the missing people were still active, and they could have been turned off. According to the Daily Mail, the crew's phones were active until the end.[71]

What does it mean? Since the phones were ringing, it means that they could receive calls, and therefore were not drowned in the sea. The range of the GSM network at 900 MHz under normal conditions is 35 km. Of course, the phone can pick up a signal from a transmitter much further away, but it is impossible to talk - this is usually the case at sea. It follows from the above that it is possible that the phones of the missing passengers were on land[72], where there was GSM coverage, or in its immediate vicinity - in Malaysia or Vietnam. So we understand the frustration of the others - since the phones work and mobile network operators are able to track them with

---

ringing-Family-members-claim-loved-ones-smartphones-active.html
[71] „19 families of missing claim to be connected - airline have also called crew." - https://www.dailymail.co.uk/news/article-2578020/Why-cellphones-missing-Malaysian-Airlines-passengers-ringing-Family-members-claim-loved-ones-smartphones-active.html
[72] or in the air

an accuracy of several meters, the authorities must know where the missing are. And that's what ...

31.6. ...caused great emotions

However, the situation becomes more complicated when we have to take into account the fact that cell phones are to be switched off on board, which, whether inadvertently or intentionally, some travelers didn't do. Or maybe for some reason they turned on the phones, but the question immediately arises why didn't they answer the incoming calls?

Attempts to connect with passengers on the missing flight MH-370 continued for three days after their disappearance. Smartphone batteries could be charged for about two or three days, but of ordinary phones, up to weeks. But this is all in the event that these devices don't fall into the salt water that would deactivate them in a short time.

According to the rescuers, this fact results in several possibilities, namely:

For unknown reasons, the plane landed in a place with cellular coverage. The phones ring, but their owners cannot accept the call. Perhaps they don't even have their phones with them. This possibility indicates a kidnapping.

The plane fell to the ground or into the sea near the coast. Some telephones were in luggage and survived the fall, and then floated on the surface of the sea, or withstood a fall to the ground, for example to a forest or mangroves.

The plane fell apart at a cruising altitude of 11,000 m, and air currents could transfer luggage containing mobile phones turned on to a place within the range of the GSM telephone network.

The passengers' cell phones responding to calls were left at home or at their workplace.

Travelers who were called on their phones had them diverted to other cellular or telephone lines.

The operator China Mobile, which has almost 800 million users and is the largest mobile operator in the world, tried to track the cells at the request of family members of the disaster victims and the Chinese government unfortunately to no avail[73].

In addition, Malaysian Boeing-777s are not equipped with satellite phones, ergo such option is also impossible.

---

[73] LUK, Lorraine: „China Mobile: Not Able to Locate Cellphones on Missing Malaysia Plane" -
https://blogs.wsj.com/digits/2014/03/13/china-mobile-not-able-to-locate-cellphones-on-missing-malaysia-plane/

The possibility that travelers' cell phones logged into the network while flying over land at an altitude of 11,000 m depends on so many factors that it is mostly coincidence. From time to time, it will be possible to deliver an SMS to a phone, usually with information about roaming or a contact with the embassy in a given country. GSM transmitters are not intended for transmission "into the sky", but the probability of logging into the network increases at low flight altitudes. Even in this case, however, it does not imply the ability to speak, due to the speed of the aircraft as well as the lack of signal coverage at normal flight level. However, under certain circumstances it is possible to send a short text message, but if it was a hijacking and the perpetrators were ready, they could use a mobile signal jammer in the immediate vicinity of the cockpit or directly in it. Indeed, this illegal device can be purchased on the Asian black market for only a few dozen euros. From a technical point of view, it would only be sufficient to delete the 900 MHz band, which would not affect other air communication systems operating at much lower frequencies (ACARS, HF and VHF). Then you cannot log in to the phone.

However, if something like this had been done during the flight of the MH-370, logging in to at least one cell phone would have solved the puzzle around the trajectory of the aircraft. One registration of the device in the network is enough to check whether the missing Boeing flew north or south from the Strait of Malacca. However, there are limitations that decrease the usefulness of this procedure. Cell phones should be turned off on board, and flight attendants are clearly instructed to do so prior to take-off. Nevertheless, it is hoped that at least some of the 237 passengers didn't do so, but that is not yet a win in terms of data evaluation. Operators store data after logging into the network for a limited period of several dozen hours, then it is removed from the system due to capacity reasons.

During the investigation, was also considered the detection of an emergency signal from the ELT (Emergency Locator Transmitter), which was also on board the missing plane. Beacons are automatically activated in the event of an emergency landing or accident on land or at sea, and are even permanently built into emergency slides and inflatable boats. At 406 MHz, they communicate with the Cospas-Sarsat satellites in low orbit. Theoretically, in the event of a hijacking, cabin crew may not notice the position of the aircraft, but their members are not trained for this eventuality as it is assumed that the beacons will be used outside the aircraft during an emergency landing.

31.7. From China to the Andaman Sea

Already in the first days of the search, the Malay Ministry of Communication and Transport began to check, based on the data from radar observations, whether the pilots, due to some problem, had wanted to change their course and return to the take-off airport. In such a case, would have to be expanded the search area, which already after a few days included 90,000 km^2 of parts of the Gulf of Thailand, the Strait of Malacca, the South China Sea and the Andaman Sea. And if the plane continued its flight for a few hours after radio contact was lost, its wreckage would be hundreds if not thousands of kilometers away - in an area stretching from India to Australia.

Rescue teams from 9 countries joined the search, unfortunately it didn't bring any result. The crew of a Vietnamese Navy plane noticed an object at the southern coast of Vietnam that looked like a door from a missing plane, and later suspicious objects floating on the waves[74] were

[74] HRADECKY, Simon: „Crash: Malaysia B772 over Gulf of Thailand on Mar 8th 2014, aircraft missing, data indicate flight MH-370 ended west of Australia, first MH-370 debris identified, search ended." - http://avherald.com/h?article=4710c69b&opt=0

photographed, which raised hope after it turned out that the oil stain found by Vietnamese airmen was, according to the CNN report[75], only oil used on large cargo ships.

The already difficult situation surrounding the search, involving 43 ships and 40 aircraft from more than a dozen countries, was further complicated by contradictory statements by the Malaysian aviation authorities and the military, according to which, the plane could be turned back from the last known position between Malaysia and Vietnam. However, how the pilots of such a large plane (over 60 meters long, wingspan of 64 meters and a maximum take-off weight of almost 300 tons) could do so without being tracked by ground radars remains a mystery. Theoretically, it can be assumed that the plane flew somewhere under the radar, but practically it's almost impossible. For example, when military pilots are trained to perform similar maneuvers, their machines have on board devices enabling them to fly at extremely low altitudes[76], or apparatus to disrupt or deceive enemy radar systems. Of course, neither of them are aboard the civilian Boeing-777, so its crew has no control over whether or not it is visible on radar

---

[75] SAEED, Ahmed – SHOICHET, Catherine: „'There are no answers': Days later, no sign of Malaysia Airlines Flight 370." -
https://edition.cnn.com/2014/03/10/world/asia/malaysia-airlines-plane/index.html

[76] Below 200 m

screens. In addition, large planes flying so low, just a few hundred meters above sea level, would be dangerous.[77]

And yet the plane became invisible in the exact sense of the word. As it turned out, the plane was still communicating with the satellites 5 hours after it had lost communication with Malaysia's air traffic control. It is therefore very likely that the plane flew northwest to the Bay of Bengal or southwest to the Indian Ocean for another five hours and crashed. An evaluation of the satellite data would allow the approximate position of the aircraft to be determined at the last contact.

The head of the Malaysian Civil Aviation Agency, Azharuddin Abdul Rahman, said at a press conference that a skyjacking is also under consideration. This option was later confirmed by the Malaysian government. Prime Minister Najib Razak, according to the BBC, ruled out that the plane had crashed due to a technical malfunction because someone intentionally had disabled the plane's communications systems while traveling from the South China Sea to the west.

"Based on satellite information, we can confidently say that the ACARS air communication system stopped working shortly before the machine reached the eastern coast of the Malaysian Peninsula," said the Prime Minister, quoted by The Star[78]. Soon

---

[77] However, a flight over the sea could explain why the plane was not tracked by airport radars on its course.

after, Air Force ground personnel spotted the plane, but only as a dot on the main radar as it could not be more accurately identified by the transponder on board the plane. This unknown object then turned west. The Malaysian authorities from the very beginning assumed that it was the missing Boeing, but were reluctant to confirm the information. "Despite media reports of the hijacking of the plane, I would like to clarify that we are still investigating all possible causes that could have led to a change of the direction of MH370 flight," Prime Minister Razak said. One Malaysian government official involved in the investigation told reporters that the plane was likely hijacked by a hijacker or group of hijackers with pilot experience. However, no motive of such act appeared and no demands were made - which has been true even after many years.

31.8. They flew away into the unknown

The distance a Boeing-777 can cover depends on its speed, which officially equals 900 km/h, altitude, wind direction, strength, and many other factors. So if the instruments were

---

[78] Najib: „MH370 deviated but no confirmation on hijacking" - https://www.thestar.com.my/News/Nation/2014/03/15/Najib-No-confirmation-missing-MH370-hijacked/

sending data to the satellites for four more hours after the plane disappeared from the secondary ground radar screens, it could have flown another three and a half thousand kilometers. If it was moving in the direction of the wind, it would have been a few hundred kilometers more, otherwise less. Let's try to count together. The plane flew regularly between Kuala Lumpur and Beijing at a distance of about 4,500 kilometers. After losing contact, it flew about 500 kilometers. Although the range of the Boeing 777-200ER is up to 14,000 kilometers with full tanks, the plane was underfilled and had fuel for approximately 5,500 kilometers, which was enough for the designated route.

We can only assume that the Boeing had been flying for four hours in an unknown direction since losing radar contact, until it crashed due to lack of fuel, but we must take into account that it hadn't have to fly at the ideal altitude of eleven kilometers, and the fuel consumption had been somewhat higher. In the moment of silence, the plane must have had enough fuel in the tank for 4,500 to 5,000 kilometers, or 5 to 6 hours of flight time, and not just four, as some authors mistakenly believed. Of course, the plane could crash for other reasons as well, due to a failure or an emergency landing. If we look at a map, we can see that the plane could approach or even reach the northern coast of Australia by flying over the Pacific Ocean towards the Philippines, or in other direction, far into the Indian Ocean. Towards the north, its trajectory would have led deep into India, central China and even the Himalayas. This would answer the question of why no remains were found in the South China Sea. Despite the fact that its waters are not deep and there is lively sea traffic, searchers couldn't find anything because there was nothing.

Already three days after the plane's disappearance, spontaneously unverified information appeared that the flight of the MH-370 was seen by the military radar system in the Strait of Malacca during strange maneuvers after losing control of the flight, which was later confirmed. Indeed, an analysis of the data provided by the Malaysian side from the Kota Bahru and Butterworth radar stations showed that the plane, after a significant change to the original course to Beijing, had climbed from the standard flight altitude of 11,000 meters, 2,700 meters higher, or even 600 meters more than the manufacturer of the Boeing 777-200ER aircraft assumed. Then the plane flew over the island of Penang, located in the Strait of Malacca, and at the same time, for unknown reasons, fell to a low flight altitude of 7,000 meters. Then it climbed back to its normal flight altitude and changed course from south-west to north-west, reaching the corridor eastward - to India and Europe. However, it is also possible that pilots over the Andaman Sea headed further northwest along the corridor or southwest into the southern Indian Ocean.

Investigators only used data from the service communication of Rolls-Royce engines with the service post (the so-called pings), from which it was possible to indirectly deduce the distance of the plane from the satellite and confirm that it had changed course.

On March 14, 2014, investigators announced that, according to radar records, the plane had indeed sharply changed its original course from the north-east, and turned west. It flew north over Malaysia, and on the border with Thailand near the island of Phuket, it entered the air corridor to Europe or the Middle East. The last radar contact with it was to take place over the Andaman Islands.

Soon after, representatives of the British satellite operator Immarsat confirmed that the plane was equipped with a satellite communication system, which, even after the machine disappeared from the radar screens, sent several short messages until it was deactivated for unknown reasons.

Let's try to put together the information known to us and tell the story of the ghost plane with the words of the Czech author Jan Matura, which after six years have not lost anything of their relevance:

The Malaysia Airlines Boeing 777-200ER headed in the right direction, to Beijing over Malaysia's east coast. Someone, possibly the pilots, turned off one of the communication systems (ACARS) as early as 40 minutes after take-off, but the pilots stopped communicating with flight control 1h 20m after departure, leaving Malaysia airspace and reporting to Vietnam Control. From that moment on, the flight MH-370 became a ghost plane. According to data from the Malaysian military radar, the machine turned sharply westwards, and along the northern border of Malaysia, it flew southwest to nowhere, to the island of Penang on the west coast of Malaysia. There the plane turned northwest and from the Strait of Malacca headed for the Andaman Islands. However, the last picking up of the signal by primary (passive) radar happened before they were reached. To illustrate the situation, let's say this area is not the end of the Earth. The plane flew near international airports in Langkawi, Penang, Phuket, as well as Kuala Lumpur and Singapore.[79]

We agree with the author that it is very strange that near international airports, which serve tens of millions of passengers per year, in a crowded air corridor, no one noticed the missing ghost plane:

Apparently no one noticed the plane, except for Malaysian radar. Neither Thais, Indonesians from Sumatra, nor Indians in the Andaman Islands. The plane wasn't registered even by

---

[79]   MATURA, Jan: „Letadlo duchů si to štrádovalo po Asii jako o nedělní vycházce" - https://www.idnes.cz/technet/technika/zmizeni-boeing-777-200er-malaysia-airlines-mh370.A140316_221604_tec_technika_jm

the main civil air traffic radars and individual airports. According to this data, the spectral pilot (whoever he was) knew well what he was doing. There were also reports that the plane had flown very low for part of the flight to hide from radars. Theoretically, it could have gone north through the corridor or, as some theories suggest, it could have flown over the center of Sumatra and into the Indian Ocean, and then headed south. But it is not yet clear, nor do we know the motive as to why this all happened. At a time when it is debated around the world how different authorities can track almost anyone in the world, because every cell phone almost perfectly maps the movement of people, as well as how different security forces monitor almost the whole world using satellites and piloted and unmanned aerial vehicles, ghost planes are an unprecedented event.[80]

31.9. The unsuccessful search

Already at an early stage, Low Earth Orbit satellites - LEO were involved in the search for the missing aircraft in an area of 93,000 km², which can be compared to the surface of Hungary. The government agency "New China" quite optimistically

---

[80] Ibidem

informed that the Chinese satellite photographed a probable crash site. Three suspect floating objects could be seen on the surface of the sea in the photos viewed by specialists, according to information provided by CNN[81]. The photos were taken on March 9, so one day after the plane disappeared from the radars at the coordinates: N06°42'- E105°37'48" - north-east from Kuala Lumpur and near the southern tip of the border of Vietnam[82]. Malaysian, Vietnamese and Indian planes were heading to this point in the South China Sea, but none of them came across any incriminated items.

India has also joined the search with its naval and air forces deployed at bases in the Andamanda and Nicobar Islands, which number 1,500 islands, of which only 400 are inhabited. In mid-March 2014, it could be said that the rescue operation undertaken by 14 countries of this region ended in failure.

Bloomberg has now reported that satellites spotted the Boeing of flight MH-370 over the Indian Ocean, about 1,600 km west of Perth, Australia[83]. The searchers therefore changed

---

[81] BOTELHO, Greg – MULLEN Jethro – PEARSON, Michael: „Satellite looking into missing Malaysia flight detects 'suspected crash area'." - https://edition.cnn.com/2014/03/12/world/asia/malaysia-airlines-plane/index.html

[82] The map shows that this point is almost exactly in the middle between Malaysia and Vietnam, and therefore it's ideal for some avoidance or escape maneuver ...

their search area, and, according to the BBC, moved to an area over which there is a busy air corridor between Southeast Asia and the Middle East[84]. It begins in the airspace of Kazakhstan, then crosses Turkmenistan to Thailand. A further possibility where the missing Boeing may have flown is the southern airway corridor that passes through the southern Indian Ocean to Indonesia. The search area has expanded considerably!

31.10. Unsaid radar data

In the course of the search, some week later, incredible reports came to light. The missing plane was observed not only by Malaysian but also Thai radars. The Thai people admitted it later, when the Malaysians asked them - only after 9 days. According to the marshal Monthon Suchookorn, Thai radars spotted the Boeing already during its flight over the South China Sea at 01:28 am MYT, i.e. 00:28 am ICT, which matches

---

[83] LEVIN, Alan – KHARIF, Olga: „Missing Malaysian Jet Said Tracked to Ocean Off Australia" - https://www.bloomberg.com/news/articles/2014-03-14/india-looking-for-malaysian-jet-as-u-s-sees-air-piracy

[84] „Missing Malaysia Airlines plane 'deliberately diverted'" - https://www.bbc.com/news/world-asia-26591056

the chronology of events leading up to the disappearance of MH-370, as noted by the Australian daily ABC[85].

The second radar record from the Andaman Sea north-west from Malaysia, the Thai offices had kept for themselves for a period of 9 days, and later justified it saying that the Malaysians hadn't asked about it. Taking into account this new information, the Thai Army forwarded these records to members of the commission of inquiry on March 17. According to the marshal Suchookorn, the missing plane didn't invade or even head for Thai airspace, and the Thai people could only guess who it belonged to as it was unidentified.

Initially, there was speculation that the Thai radar was intentionally disabled during the incident, as was the Indian radar in the Andaman Islands. Even Malaysia claimed that some radar stations were not active at night. Indonesia, which owns the Sumatra radar stations whose data may be of interest, hasn't reported it at all. The AV Herald news site referenced the words of a senior Malaysian official who said that the delayed communication between the Thai and Malaysian armies was merely media speculation[86]. As both countries were informed

---

[85] McDONELL, Stephen – EDWARDS, Michael: „Malaysia Airlines flight MH370: Thailand detected missing jet minutes after it changed course" - https://www.abc.net.au/news/2014-03-19/malaysia/5332052

[86] HRADECKY, Simon: Crash: „Malaysia B772 over Gulf of Thailand on Mar 8th 2014, aircraft missing, data indicate flight MH-370 ended

that the plane had been flying in a different direction since the last contact, the first week wasn't wasted on a search of the Gulf of Thailand.

The suspension, if not the immediate impediment of the collaboration, that characterized the search for missing planes at the time, was the logical, although overly sad result of the inadequacy of political leadership in the South China Sea. But if Malaysia initially refused to publish the source data from its radar because of the "over-sensitivity" of that information, it's no wonder - the speed at which radars can monitor an area allows a fairly accurate estimate of the level of advanced technology used. It is therefore possible that even today, in 2020, some countries may still have MH-370 radar data after the transponder has been turned off, but will not provide information so that other countries cannot assess their defense capabilities and jeopardize their national interests. We can even imagine the possibility that the submarines patrolling the South China Sea have noticed something unusual, such as the plane crashing to the surface or its wreck on the seabed, but disclosing this information would only reveal the simple fact that the aircraft has been found there.

---

west of Australia, first MH-370 debris identified, search ended" - http://avherald.com/h?article=4710c69b&opt=0

Meanwhile, there was crazy speculation about what might have happened to the MH-370. It was unclear how looked the first maneuver after which the plane traveled west of its original route, and although it was captured by two countries' radars, its precise movement in this area remained a mystery. Comments were made that due to a technical failure, pilots could go to Langkawi Airport in the Strait of Malacca, to which the runway is directly accessible by sea. According to this interpretation, the plane wouldn't have returned to Kuala Lumpur as it would have had Cameron Heights with peaks of nearly two kilometers before itself. However, when we look at the maps, in an emergency the pilots would have had one of two airports to choose, in Kota Bahru on the east coast of Malaysia, and other with a sufficiently long runway for an emergency landing in Kuala Terenggate. All this in a triangle with the length of the sides equaling about five hundred kilometers.

And to make the confusion even worse, the American TV station Fox News quoted General Thomas McInerney, according to which the missing plane landed in Pakistan[87].

31.11. The last signal from the cockpit

---

[87] Lt. Gen. McInerney: „Flight 370 Could Have Landed in Pakistan" - https://insider.foxnews.com/2014/03/18/lt-gen-mcinerney-flight-370-could-have-landed-pakistan

The investigation into the missing flight MH-370 didn't omit the last signal from the cockpit of the missing plane. The last words of the radio correspondence from the missing machine were "Okay, I understand," the BBC reported[88]. In the media appeared also other version presented by the Malaysian Ambassador to Beijing: "All right, good night." According to News, one of the pilots should have relaxed as the plane flew from Malaysian into Vietnamese airspace. Investigators noted that the pilot at the time must have known about the disconnection of the ACARS Identification System. They made an important remark: "It's just the perfect place to disappear, it would have been too strange a coincidence."[89]

The Telegraph daily on January 29, 2015 published a copy of the last hour of radio correspondence, which the pilots had kept with the control tower, and which we provide in full. The time

---

[88] „Malaysia Airlines MH370: Last communication revealed" - https://www.bbc.com/news/world-asia-26541057

[89] WOCKNER, Cindy: „Malaysia under fire over chaotic search into missing flight MH370" - https://www.news.com.au/malaysia-under-fire-over-chaotic-search-into-missing-flight-mh370/news-story/7cef815a447d998ab1013d383f18a08d It should be added that it was then that the Malaysian Boeing was in the middle of the South China Sea - an ideal place for an escape or avoidance maneuver...

used is MYT. Air traffic controllers are marked as ATC, and the missing plane is MH-370.

Radio communication with the Kuala Lumpur Air Traffic Control Tower:

Time: 00:36.30 am - establishing communication.

MH-370: Air Traffic Control, this is MH-370, good morning! (the plane makes contact with the control tower before take-off)

ATC: Good morning, MH-370, this is Kuala Lumpur control tower. Please wait for the A-10, 32-R (the plane is to wait in position until it is directed to one of the two runways marked as 14-L or 32-R)

Time 00:36.50 am
MH-370: A-10, I understand.

Time 00:38.43 am - begin of the aircraft starting run on the A-10/14-L runway.

ATC: MH-370, please move to the runway (the plane has been cleared to go to the runway starting place)

MH-370: To the A-10 runway, we get it.

Time: 00: 40.38 am

ATC: MH-370, runway 32-R is free, take off allowed. Good night.

MH-370: The runway 32-R is free, we have clearance. We understand, thank you and goodbye. (the plane confirms permission to take off)

Time: 00:42.05 am

MH-370: MH-370 leaves the airport space.

Time: 00:42.10 am

ATC: MH-370, we confirm your position, flight altitude 180, follow the instructions and turn right to IGARI waypoint (the plane is instructed to achieve 18,000 ft/5500 m altitude and take course to IGARI waypoint in the South China Sea around halfway between Malaysia and Vietnam)

Time: 00:42:40 am

MH-370: All right, flight altitude 180, IGARI waypoint. (A commenter from The Telegraph acknowledges that the pilot communicates informally.)

Time: 00:42:52 am - further dialogue with the control tower

ATC: MH-370, Kuala Lumpur radar is taking you over, frequency 132.6, good night (They notify the flight crew that they have left the airport area and that they are to switch to the area control frequency, which maintains communication between flight endpoints.) MH-370: We understand, 132.6.

Communication with the area control:

Time: 00:46.51 am

MH-370: Kuala Lumpur Airspace Control, this is MH-370!

ATC: MH-370, please ascend to 250 m (call for altitude increase to 7,600 m)

Time 00:46.54 am

MH-370: MH-370 goes to ceiling 250 (airplane goes to its higher flight altitude)

Time: 00: 50.06 am

ATC: MH-370, achieve altitude 350 (plane enters travel altitude of 11,700 m)

Time: 00:50.09 am

MH-370: Ceiling 350.

Time 01: 01.14 am

MH-370: We're at ceiling 350.

Time: 01:07:55 am

MH-370: We maintain the altitude of 350. (Pilot confirms after 6 minutes. The plane maintains the set flight altitude.)

Time 01:19:24 am

ATC: MH-370, please contact Ho Shi Minh on frequency 120.9. Good night! (The plane approaches the Vietnamese airspace. Malaysian controllers give it a new frequency and connect)

Time: 01:19:24 am - the last communication

MH-370: All right, good night! (The copilot Fariq Abdul Hamid used loose words instead of a business formula.)

Further communication broke off.

On March 31, 2014, the Malaysian Civil Aviation Authority announced that the last words between the tower and the missing plane were not "All right, good night," but "Okay, Malaysian three seven zero." This, however, does not change the events in any way, because the analysts working on the text of the talks considered this statement to be routine. However, they indicated two moments as "potentially strange". The first one was a report at 01:07 am, repeating the information already provided that the plane was maintaining a level of 10,700 meters (35,000 ft), at the exact same time that the plane automatically sent an engine condition report via the ACARS communication system. Within the next thirty minutes, ACARS was turned off - according to the Investigative Committee, apparently before the pilot's last communication with the ground staff, after which the transponder was silent (turned off). The second suspicious moment indicates that communication was terminated at the junction of the two airspaces, i.e. on site and at the time it was to be given over to the Vietnamese by the Malaysian dispatchers. "If I wanted to steal the plane, I would do it there," former Boeing-777 pilot Stephen Buzdygan told The Telegraph.[90]

And one more strange thing. The Malaysian Ministry of Transport released a complete record of the pilots' conversations with the tower only on 27 May 2014. The declassified 47-page transcript contains the routine exchange of

---

[90] PEARLMAN, Jonathan: „MH370: Analysis of the last 54 minutes of communication from the plane" -
https://www.telegraph.co.uk/news/worldnews/asia/malaysia/1071519
5/MH370-Analysis-of-the-last-54-minutes-of-communication-from-
the-plane.html

signals between aircraft and satellites after communications systems went silent.

But if the data had been released earlier, it might have helped find the lost plane. "There are a lot of irrelevant things, and about two or three pages are really serious," said satellite communications expert Michael Exner. "It is mainly data from the Inmarsat satellite. But it lacks the accompanying metadata and algorithms, without which the correctness of the Inmarsat scientists' calculations cannot be satisfactorily verified. The document answers many questions, but a lot remains open."[91] CNN news analyst David Soucie also agreed: "There is not enough information to allow independent experts to scrutinize the results of the investigation."[92]

The parade of inconsistencies and mysteries therefore continues.

[91] WELCH, William: „Malaysia releases Flight 370 raw satellite data" - https://eu.usatoday.com/story/news/usanow/2014/05/26/mh370-data-to-be-released/9603371/

[92] MULLEN, Jethro – MOHSIN, Saima: „Malaysia Airlines Flight 370: Satellite data released after long wait" - https://edition.cnn.com/2014/05/27/world/asia/malaysia-missing-plane/

31.12. About pilots, kidnappers and organs selling

Among other options, an investigation into the mysterious flight MH-370 also involved the aircraft's captain, Zaharie Ahmad Shah, 53, and co-pilot Fariq Abdul Hamid, 27. The captain was an employee of the company for over three decades. He was one of the most experienced pilots, and his hobby was to fly virtually using the flight simulator he owned. Both men's mail boxes were checked by the police in addition to house searches. The investigators also checked if the captain had trained flight maneuvers en route from Beijing, or shutting down key systems responsible for locating the plane.

And investigators came to the surprising discovery that Zaharie Ahmad Shah had been piloting the plane on his computers to remote areas of the South Indian Ocean just one month before the MH-370 mysterious disappearance, New York magazine wrote. Malaysian experts transferred to the FBI computers, the hard drives on which Zaharie recorded the routes processed in a home flight simulator. Recovered data revealed that the captain flew northwest from Kuala Lumpur through the Strait of Malacca, then turned left and headed south over the Indian Ocean until the plane ran out of fuel.

The signals picked up by the satellites indicate that the actual route of flight MH370 before disappearing, was very similar. It wasn't exactly the same, but in both cases it ended up very far away from populated areas. According to journalists, this may be the most serious indication that it could have been a mass murder and suicide committed by the plane pilots.[93]

This is undoubtedly a strong objection, but it cannot be dismissed lightly, even though it may seem absurd at first from the standpoint of Zaharie's privacy and great career. The captain had a decent financial income of $8,000 per month, and he and his family lived in above-standard conditions. He had three adult children, including one daughter who studied at a university abroad. His career was flawless, and at first glance there is no indication of a potential hijacking or suicide inclination that would have caused the death of the passengers and crew. On the other hand, the media reported that in addition to frustration or depression caused by the divorce, also his political convictions could be a motive, because - as we already mentioned - he was an opposition supporter, and opposition leader Anwar Ibrahim was probably sentenced to five years in prison. The press also mentioned about a mysterious phone call that the captain received from an

---

[93] The so-called extended suicide as in the case of the Germanwings 9525 aircraft, whose second pilot in a state of depression deliberately directed the plane to the slope of an alpine mountain in France, on March 24, 2015.

unknown woman. She used a disposable SIM card purchased with fake papers.[94]

Some journalists speculated that Zaharie was a relatively important opposition political activist, so the captain could theoretically do something bad, but why on earth would have he done it? First Officer Fariq Abdul Hamid was young and was shortly before his wedding. His fiancée also worked as a pilot on Air Asia planes and, as far as we know, he wasn't in an emotional state that would make him harm himself and other passengers. This is true despite the fact that the imagination of the readers of tabloid novels allows us to imagine a situation where the impending wedding would have had to be canceled, and the jealous, screaming fiancé would have decided to put an end to it for good.

Larry Vance, an expert in Canada, came up with an explanation that one of the pilots could take the plane to the sea with suicide intentions. Similar tragic events took place in the past, but remain taboo. A pilot in Mozambique crashed the plane to the ground in 2013. There is a known tragic case of an

---

[94] PARRY, Simon: „Police hunt mystery woman who made final phone call to doomed jet captain as first picture emerges of his estranged wife and family." - https://www.dailymail.co.uk/news/article-2587064/Probe-mystery-call-captain-doomed-jet-Unknown-woman-used-fake-ID-buying-phone-bypass-security-checks.html

Egyptian pilot who in 1999 directed a plane flying from New York to Cairo, into the waters off the US coast. Silk Air flight from Jakarta to Singapore ended with suicide in 1997, and that's not all. Investigators and officials are reluctant to admit that the pilot may intentionally cause the plane to crash with passengers - even if the evidence was more than convincing. However, Vance's theory outlined in his new book[95] was strongly rejected by Peter Foley of the Australian Aviation Safety Authority.

A likely motive is missing even in the case of a skyjacking. Al-Qaida-related terrorist groups from Malaysia and Indonesia were dispersed years ago, and hijacking assumes some results that don't exist here. The plane has not yet been found, it disappeared without witnesses in a remote area. There is no scenario that would have allowed to demand a ransom, political concessions, someone's release from prison. Also an empty but direct terrorist gesture should be excluded. If it was a crime, there were no more witnesses, no one to intimidate the culprit. Despite these reservations, ex-pilot Randy Ryan still tries to find evidence of the hijacking of the plane. He mainly uses the fact that the transponder stopped responding.[96]

---

[95] VANCE, Larry: „MH370: Mystery Solved", Group of Three Publishing, Plano, 2018

[96] In the event of a kidnapping or terrorist act, the kidnappers or terrorists usually make their demands up to 72 hours after the

This possibility was also confirmed by experts at the Royal Air Company Air Operations Group conference, attended by pilots, airline representatives, aircraft manufacturers and supervisory officials.[97] They also focused on explaining how to disable the ACARS communication system, which transmits on-board technical data to ground stations via radio or satellite. According to experts, the shutdown of the system that took place on the MH-370 is possible, but requires quite complex knowledge and cannot be done from the cockpit. And conversely, switching off the transponder identifying the aircraft on the secondary radars can be done directly in the cockpit. The transponder is usually turned off after landing. On this basis, experts convened by the Royal Aeronautics Company confirmed that the shutdown of ACARS was intentional and could have been caused by a hijacking.

"It couldn't be a coincidence. At the same time, I don't think it was an amateur job," says Ryan, who claims the perpetrators must have been professionals. "The aircraft hijackers knew how to avoid detection. The pilot and co-pilot were doing what they usually did. They took off, set a course, and let the autopilot guide. Suddenly the transponder stopped responding. This is

---

incident. In the event of the MH-370, this was not the case, so this hypothesis doesn't make sense.

[97] READ, Bill: „What happened to flight MH370?" - https://www.aerosociety.com/news/what-happened-to-flight-mh370/

no coincidence, pilots know that without it you can fly out of radar range."[98]

Former Fox News reporter Darlene Tipton has recently made the truly terrifying hypothesis that airplane hijackers had sold their passengers to human organ traffickers in China, and she currently prepares a document on this subject.[99] According to her, all victims of this organ harvesting scheme were Falun Gong practitioners who had their body parts removed as part of an 'on demand' organ transplant scheme for rich people. "I hope that China arrests Falun Gong practitioners and stop the heinous act of using these prisoners of conscience to facilitate China's inexcusable and horrendous practice of live organ harvesting," Tipton said.[100] Of the 239 passengers on board, 153 were of Chinese nationality. However, the importance of this

---

[98] PERKINS, Liz: „Pilot calls for a fresh search for missing jet MH370 around Madagascar as he claims the doomed flight was hijacked before it vanished in 2014 with 239 people on board." - https://www.dailymail.co.uk/news/article-6635473/Pilot-calls-new-search-missing-MH370-Madagascar-claims-flight-hijacked.html

[99] IKONEN, Charlotte: „MH370 mystery solved? Former TV exec has 'PROOF' linking disappearance to organ harvesting." - https://www.dailystar.co.uk/news/world-news/mh370-flight-news-malaysia-airlines-16825956

[100] VARANDANI, Suman: „MH370 Hijacked For Organ Harvesting, New Conspiracy Theory Claims." - https://www.ibtimes.com/mh370-hijacked-organ-harvesting-new-conspiracy-theory-claims-2743000

claim is undermined by the fact that China was one of the most active countries involved in the search, it spent tens of millions of dollars and sent rescuers, planes and ships. Darlene Tipton worked for Fox News for over two decades. She was dismissed shortly after she had used a corporate email address to organize a fundraiser for relatives of MH-370 victims.

31.13. Mayday! Explosion and fire on board

One of the most common causes of plane crashes are fires on board. A possible scenario was presented by CNN[101]. A Boeing-777 pilot Les Abend said that the plane had begun to burn for unknown reasons, and the pilots had wanted to direct the plane to one of the airports in Langkawi, Penang or Kuala Lumpur. This is also indicated by changes in the course and flight level. After the fire and smoke intensified, the crew ran out of oxygen in the breathing apparatus. The autopilot-controlled plane was flying northwest, towards India. However, one of the engines stopped working due to the fire, making the plane turn south and fly along Sumatra to the Indian Ocean, west of Australia. The telescopic generator powered the system

---

[101] ABEND, Les: „How mechanical problem could have downed Flight 370." - https://edition.cnn.com/2014/03/24/opinion/abend-explaining-flight-370/index.html

until the plane fell into the sea. However, this hypothesis has one big catch - it doesn't explain the shutdown of the aviation communications systems. While it is possible that flames in the electronics department could cause this, it is unlikely that the Boeing continued to fly for a few more hours at a relatively stable course, without changing it.

We also need to take into account the situation when the plane reaches the last entered route waypoint, and the next point isn't entered. This is an important question because the Boeing flew over several course points after a course change, and the last recorded position was in the Andaman Sea - the plane came to it from the south, and was heading north-west. Experts agreed on two options. It was as if the plane had been stopped at that moment: they continued the course or began to circle around the last waypoint. But it doesn't explain why the plane then traveled south, so neither of these variants are valid.

In addition to the destructive power of fire, we can also consider decompression, possibly as a result of a fire in the cargo area or a detonation of an explosive. A catastrophic scenario would remind us of fighting the flames. If decompression had occurred at a flight level of 11 kilometers, people without oxygen masks would have survived a maximum of one minute, then it would have caused irreversible brain damage and death. Passengers with oxygen masks can breathe for about a quarter, and pilots with oxygen cylinders for much longer. The crew attempted to divert the plane to an emergency airport, which apparently failed, and the autopilot-navigated plane then flew south towards the Indian Ocean. In the event that the plane wasn't destroyed immediately, it is really strange that the crew didn't send an emergency signal, and the ACARS system was shut down.

Decompression is also considered according to the script of the best-selling writer Thomas H. Block, Mayday. It describes the flight of a supersonic transport plane which was accidentally hit by a missile fired during an exercise. The board was swept by decompression that immediately killed the crew and some of the passengers, and only a few people which were in the toilets of the plane further controlled by autopilot, escaped this fate.

In the case of the MH370 flight, we cannot rule out damage to the aircraft's fuselage caused by an anti-aircraft missile, because just two months after the disappearance of the aircraft, the book about it reached the readers.[102] Its author Nigel Cawthorne explains that the Boeing was accidentally shot down during a joint exercise of the Thai and US armies, and that the search for rubble was just a masked maneuver.[103]

---

[102] CAWTHORNE, Nigel: „Flight MH370 The Mystery", John Blake Publishing, London, 2014

[103] PEARLMAN, Jonathan: „MH370: author's claims Malaysia

"The maneuvers included a simulated battle on land, air and water, as well as live ammunition fire. Admittedly, the participants accidentally shot down the flight MH-370. Something like that happens, no one wants another Lockerbie, so culprits have many reasons to hide it," says the British writer, according to whom it is suspected that no black boxes have yet been found. And if they are discovered, they won't be of probative value: "The investigators could throw another black box into the water while searching in the South China Sea."

Irish private researcher Noel O'Gara also believes that Boeing was shot down by a rocket, and to prove his claim, he found five witnesses who had seen the machine on fire falling into the sea.[104] "After the plane had been accidentally downed, its remains were pulled from the sea," says Noel O'Gara, according to which the Malaysian army is responsible for the incident. The soldiers knew exactly where the plane had been

---

Airlines plane accidentally shot down angers victim." - https://www.telegraph.co.uk/news/worldnews/asia/malaysia/10839030/MH370-authors-claims-Malaysia-Airlines-plane-accidentally-shot-down-angers-victim.html#source=refresh

[104] HILL, Ben: „The five witnesses who could hold the key to finding MH370: Private detective claims doomed Malaysia Airlines flight was shot down - and says a handful of people can prove it." - https://www.dailymail.co.uk/news/article-6740843/Private-detective-reveals-five-witnesses-hold-key-finding-MH370.html

shot down. One of the witnesses allegedly off the coast of Vietnam was New Zealander Mike McKay, who said: "They said they had seen the plane over the sea. The pilots tried to control it, but it fell." Latife Dalelahe told him that she had seen a plane over the sea that was supposed to be at that time in the coordinates in which the plane disappeared from the radar. O´Gara's last witnesses, two Malaysian fishermen, say the plane hit the sea near the island of Kota Bharu.

In this context, in January 2019, there was also the testimony of the Indonesian fisherman Rusli Khusmin, who, together with his crew, watched the fall of MH-370. He entered the coordinates of the impact site into a GPS device and gave it to the researchers. "We saw a plane gliding like a broken dragon. There was no sound, but black smoke came out of it. Then it hit the sea," said Khusmin, who couldn't explain why he had waited five years with this information to pass it to the authorities.[105]

A similar testimony of a "high altitude burning airplane" flying at N08°23'-E108°42' was made by a South Korean oil rig

---

[105] ALDERSLEY, Miranda: „'This is where MH370 crashed': Fisherman claims he SAW plane go down and recorded the EXACT location on GPS, saying: 'It moved like a broken kite... no noise, just smoke'." - https://www.dailymail.co.uk/news/article-6597725/Fisherman-claims-SAW-MH370-recorded-EXACT-location-GPS.html

worker in the South China Sea on March 13, 2014.[106] In early June 2014, the media published a statement by British sailor Katherine Tee, who had sailed along the Indonesian coast in March. She said that she and her husband had been watching a burning plane from the deck of a yacht. At first they thought it was a meteor, but by comparing the direction of their route with that of the missing plane, they concluded that it is possible that it had been the passenger Boeing in flames: "I saw a large plane glowing orange with dark smoke behind it."[107] The plane was flying from north to south, accompanied by two other machines.[108]

31.14. Search according to the Doppler effect

[106] OHLHEISER, Abby: „Oil Rig Worker Thinks He Saw Malaysia Air Flight 370 Go Down In Flames." -
https://www.businessinsider.com/oil-rig-worker-thinks-he-saw-malaysia-flight-in-flames-2014-3

[107] LEE, Sally: Female sailor thinks she may have spotted MH370 in the sky above the Indian Ocean on the night it disappeared. -
https://www.dailymail.co.uk/news/article-2647096/Female-sailor-thinks-spotted-MH370-sky-Indian-Ocean-night-disappeared.html

[108] This is where the rumor about the hijacking of this plane by a UFO or American fighters from the base on Diego Garcia probably came from.

But let's return to the events that helped to establish the approximate final location of the MH-370 trajectory about two weeks after the crash, based on short radio signals - pings - that the plane sent on March 8 until 08:00 am MYT. Thanks to specialists from the British company Inmarsat, the suspicion that the plane fell into the Indian Ocean was confirmed.

Experts used an innovative solution based on the fact that although the MH-370 was not communicating actively for some reason, it was communicating with satellites in orbit. The device pinged the Inmarsat 3F1 satellite every hour, and although it didn't contain any data regarding its brevity, sophisticated analysis confirmed that the MH-370 flight lasted at least five hours after leaving Malaysia's airspace.

"We took into account the Doppler effect, which describes the frequency shift caused by the movement of a satellite in orbit," Inmarsat vice president Chris McLaughlin explained. This allowed the scientists to calculate the relative speed between the satellite and the plane, and then - based on the predicted speed and repeated observation - the approximate distance of the aircraft to the satellite. "We could then use this data to estimate traffic along the North or South route. Finally, we could say with certainty that the plane had chosen the southern path of the assumed trajectory."[109]

---

[109] CURTIS, Sophie: „How British satellite company Inmarsat tracked

The plane was pinging every hour from 02:11 to 08:11 am MYT. The next hour was just silence, indicating the plane's crash, and this corresponded to an estimate of its range with the right amount of fuel in the tanks. According to the BBC[110], Inmarsat also used data from other aircraft in the region that it knew exactly how to locate, to better analyze the position, taking into account isolated signals. "We found a way to check with a single ping if the plane moves and has functional instruments. Then, using the exclusion method, comparing to other flights, we found out that the aircraft had been heading south, and its speed was 833 km/h (450 knots), but we don't know yet if the plane had slowed down due to lack of fuel," explained McLauglin.

At first glance, the Doppler effect in communication between a satellite and an aircraft can only detect the distance from the aircraft, and it is not possible to determine in which direction the aircraft flew. Theoretically it should be so, but experts were able to deduce many more facts from this phenomenon.

---

down MH370." -
https://www.telegraph.co.uk/technology/news/10719304/How-British-satellite-company-Inmarsat-tracked-down-MH370.html

[110] „UK firm behind Malaysia Airlines flight MH370 breakthrough." - https://www.bbc.com/news/uk-26720772

31.15. The Missing in the Indian Ocean

So British specialists confirmed the sad fact that was already made public at that time. "Based on the research of Inmarsat and the British investigative service AAIB[111], we can deduce that the plane ended its flight in the southern part of the Indian Ocean," said the Malaysian Minister of Transport Datuk Seri Hishammuddin Hussein at a press conference on March 24, 2014.[112]

At that time, an intensive search in the indicated ocean basin, which had excited the world audience a few days earlier, was already underway. On March 20, 2014, Australian Prime Minister Tony Abbot announced that satellites detected two large objects in the Indian Ocean (one 24 meters long and the other 5 meters long).

"There may be more in the area. This is probably the best clue we have today," said John Young of the Australian

---

[111] Air Accidents Investigation Branch.

[112] "MH370 crash: Hisham on how it was concluded that flight ended in south Indian Ocean."
https://www.thestar.com.my/news/nation/2014/03/25/mh370-crash-hishammuddin-statement

Maritime Safety Authority[113], but warned that it could also be lost containers from the decks of merchant ships.[114] On March 22, this discovery was confirmed by Chinese satellites at S44°34'-E090°08', approximately 3,170 kilometers southwest of Perth, Australia. "It's the most distant place imaginable on Earth, but if there's something there, we'll find it," Tony Abbot said of the location halfway to the barren Antarctic islands.

Australia sent there four search planes and two ships. They were joined by a Norwegian merchant ship bound for Melbourne. However, the search was hampered by strong winds, clouds and heavy rain. At that time, 18 ships, 29 aircraft and 6 helicopters were deployed to search the Indian Ocean. Part of the squadron was also the Boeing P-8 Poseidon, which is used to counter underwater and surface targets. Its main advantage is the equipment with detectors and sensors, and ability to mark the location with the help of radio buoys.[115]

---

[113] "Flight MH370: Images of ocean debris."
https://www.bbc.com/news/world-asia-26662641

[114] McDONELL, Stephen: "Missing Malaysia Airlines plane: Chinese satellites spot new possible debris from MH370."
https://www.abc.net.au/news/2014-03-22/missing-malaysia-airlines-plane-mh370-debris-china-satellites/5339092

[115] MARKS, Kathy: "MH370 search: China demands to see proof that missing Malaysia Airlines flight crashed into the sea." -
https://www.independent.co.uk/news/world/asia/missing-malaysia-airlines-flight-mh370-china-demands-to-see-proof-that-jet-crashed-

However, the search in the new area was unsuccessful, and Australian Deputy Prime Minister Warren Truss didn't rule out in front of Perth journalists the possibility that both objects had sunk there during the storm, and eventually forced the searchers to temporarily withdraw.

On March 26, 2014, after the weather had stabilized in the remote southern Indian Ocean, two ships and 12 aircraft were dispatched to gradually search an area the size of Alaska. Researchers also reported that, thanks to the satellite images, they discovered 122 floating objects spanning 400 square kilometers, that could be derived from the crashed MH-370 flight. "We are not looking for a needle in a haystack as we are still trying to figure out where that haystack is," said Australian Defense Department MP Mark Binskin from Perth about that ambitious search.[116]

Meanwhile, further analysis of data from the Thai satellite system revealed another three hundred objects in the area in question. "We discovered floating objects, perhaps more than three hundred," confirmed the director of the Thai satellite

---

into-the-sea-9215276.html

[116] MARKS, Kathy: "MH370 search: China demands to see proof that missing Malaysia Airlines flight crashed into the sea." https://www.independent.co.uk/news/world/asia/missing-malaysia-airlines-flight-mh370-china-demands-to-see-proof-that-jet-crashed-into-the-sea-9215276.html

company Anont Snidvongs.[117] Objects ranging in size from two to fifteen meters were spotted by a Thai satellite over an area of several square kilometers, about 200 kilometers from where a group of 122 objects had previously been recorded by a French satellite.

Taking into account these findings, Malaysian Prime Minister Najib Razak issued a statement that the plane almost certainly had fallen into the southern Indian Ocean and no one had survived. In such a remote and inhospitable landless area, no one can survive three weeks without help, no matter what the cause of the accident.

31.16. So close to nothing...

The South Indian Ocean is without doubt one of the most distant and inhospitable places in the world, where cruel winds lash the vast watery desert. The second Point Nemo of our globe.[118] And almost there, like at the very end of the world, thousands of kilometers from any inhabited land, as Australian

---

[117] Flight MH370: Thai satellite 'shows 300 floating objects'
https://www.bbc.com/news/world-asia-26763358

[118] This most distant point, the Ocean Pole of Unavailability, is located in the Pacific at S48°52′36″-W123°23′36 ″. Currently, there is a drop site for inactive artificial satellites and space stations.

Prime Minister Tony Abbott described this place: "as close to anything as possible,"[119] the mysterious flight MH-370 probably ended its flight with 239 people on board.

"With the exception of the crews of a few fishing vessels, the waters of the southern Indian Ocean are completely deserted. To the west, Perth is separated from the nearest mainland, the Kerguelen Islands, by thousands of kilometers of undisturbed navy blue ocean which is one of the least explored areas of the world," recalls the eminent Czech journalist Ivana Milenkovičová. "In addition to the long flight hours to the nearest continent from the probable place of impact, the search for the missing plane is made difficult by the weather. Strong storms strike the open sea with lightning, and due to the absence of land, huge masses of water can flow at these latitudes with greater force than anywhere else on our planet. It was not in vain that the sailors preferred to avoid these areas. In addition to the Malaysian plane, the deep ditches of the South Indian Ocean have buried many a sailor wishing to discover unknown lands on behalf of the empires of the time. But what the MH-370 pilots wanted as their machine blasted its way through strong winds heading somewhere south into

---

[119] „Search for MH370 resumes in area 'as close to nowhere as it's possible to be'" - https://www.thejournal.ie/malaysia-airlines-search-2-1381656-Mar2014/

Antarctica, thousands of kilometers from the original route, may remain a mystery forever."[120]

In March 2014, the popular reporter had no idea how her words would literally come true, especially since even the searchers who had moved 1,100 kilometers to the northeast couldn't come to terms with the word "forever." According to new data obtained from military radar, the plane flew faster than expected, so it was without fuel even earlier, and its projected range was reduced.

At the end of March, six aircraft and eight ships under the command of the Supreme Air Marshal, Angus Houston, flew to a new area of almost 320,000 square kilometers, roughly equal to the territory of Poland, with an average depth of two to four kilometers. One of the ships was the Australian warship HMAS Ocean Shield, which transported there an American black box detection device capable of detecting a signal at a depth of 6,000 meters, as well as a robotic submarine. Meanwhile, Chinese and Australian ships pulled undefined objects from the sea, but

---

[120] MILENKOVIČOVÁ, Ivana: „Tak blízko ničemu ... Let MH370 hledají na samém konci světa." -
https://www.idnes.cz/zpravy/zahranicni/patrani-po-letu-mh370-komplikuje-pocasi-a-odlehlost-oblasti.A140327_133104_zahranicni_im

after a more detailed study, they only brought disappointment - it was just fishing equipment, floats and debris.[121]

31.17. In pursuit of black boxes

When 24 days after the disappearance of MH-370, no remains could be found, the searchers and rescuers were worried because they didn't have much time. The black boxes on board have batteries capable of powering the transmitters of these recorders for only one month. After that, their power begins to drop to zero. According to unofficial data, they are able to send signals for another 2-3 weeks, but the strength of these signals gradually decreases. If they fell into a fissure or undersea canyon, it will be very difficult to find them with optical instruments or sonar.

On April 4, 2014, the crew of the British hydrographic ship HMS Echo, searching for ultrasonic signals, announced that it had picked up one signal - which, however, turned out to be a false alarm coming from a whale.

---

[121] This reservoir is located in the South Indian Ocean Vortex - a huge stain of plastic debris that confused rescuers and seekers.

The day after, on April 5, 2014, the Chinese ship Haixun 01 caught a signal corresponding to the characteristics of the signals sent by the black boxes of the missing flight MH-370, at a frequency of 37.5 kHz. "It is the signal coming from the black boxes," said Anish Patel from Dukane Seacom which manufactures the locators.

The mysterious signal was heard every second in the period of half a minute by ship crew members, who didn't manage to record it because they didn't have the equipment prepared.[122] This news also gave rise to hope. However, oceanographer Simon Boxal was skeptical in his comment to CNN, as he said that other devices also send such signals: "If this proves to be what investigators have been searching for, then the possibility of recovering the plane or at least the black boxes goes from being one in a million to almost certain," he said also adding that "it could be a false signal."[123]

The fact that the sailors from Haixun 01 really could pick up the signal from one of the black boxes is demonstrated above all by the frequency of 37.5 kHz used, which ensures the highest

---

[122] „Malaysia missing plane search China ship 'picks up signal'" - https://www.bbc.com/news/world-asia-26902127

[123] ELLIS, Ralph – MULLEN, Jethro: „Search teams investigate sounds picked up in ocean." - https://edition.cnn.com/2014/04/05/world/asia/malaysia-airlines-plane/

possible transmission quality and eliminates ocean noise. Surprisingly, however, there are two facts: the Chinese only received the signal from one box, whereas also other box was supposed to send signals, and it happened in the place beyond the ongoing search area. According to the news agency New China, the transmission was intercepted at about 25 degrees south latitude and 101 degrees east longitude, where the ocean reaches a depth of four and a half kilometers.

While waiting for new data, the crew of the Australian ship HMAS Ocean Shield, which brought a device for locating sound in the great depths, caught further transmission. "We saw the signal on the display, but we only have a sound that could be a signal from black boxes," marshal Angus Houston announced on April 1, 2014.[124]

Reuters reported that HMAS Ocean Shield was picking up signals from the north-west coast of Australia for 2½ hours until communication broke off. When the ship turned back, the signals appeared again, this time for 13 minutes, but were from two different sources. That would fit two black boxes that recorded flight parameters and cockpit conversations. The places where these signals were heard were separated by 600

---

[124] ALMASY, Steve – SHOICHET, Catherine – SAM, Ivy: „Malaysia Flight 370: New signal sounds 'just like' one from a plane's beacon." - https://edition.cnn.com/2014/04/06/world/asia/malaysia-airlines-plane/index.html

km. Based on this development, communications expert Paul Ginsberg commented on the difficulty of the search reminiscent of the proverbial search for a needle in a haystack: "It looks like we've finally found hay."[125]

On April 8, 2014, a message appeared according to which HMAS Ocean Shield detected further acoustic signals corresponding to the characteristics of signals from black boxes. Two signals, according to BBC reports, came from a depth of 4500 m.[126] "I believe we are now looking in the right place," said Angus Houston. "Thanks to the signals, we will be able to define a small area of search and within a few days we will find something at the bottom. However, to be absolutely sure that this is the final resting place of the MH-370 flight, we need a visual identification of the aircraft remains."[127]

[125] SHOICHET, Catherine – YAN, Holly – FANTZ, Ashley: „Malaysia Flight 370: New signal sounds 'just like' one from a plane's beacon." - https://edition.cnn.com/2014/04/07/world/asia/malaysia-airlines-plane/index.html

[126] Missing Malaysia plane: Search 'regains recorder signal'". - https://www.bbc.com/news/world-asia-26950387

[127] PAYNE, ED – BOTELHO, Greg: „In search for Malaysia Airlines Flight 370, two new signals buoy hope." - https://edition.cnn.com/2014/04/09/world/asia/malaysia-airlines-plane/index.html

On April 14, HMAS Ocean Shield discovered an oil spill. A 2-liter sample was taken from it for laboratory analysis. We need to establish an oil source, but it is 5.5 km against the wind from where the signals were picked up using a sound recognition device, marshal Houston announced at a press conference.[128] On April 18, the sample was ready, but the result was negative, so it wasn't from the missing plane.

The detection of signals made it possible to reduce the searched body of water to 58,000 km^2, which was a significant step, because it was a complex search due to the relief of the bottom and ocean currents. "Imagine that you are standing at the top of a mountain and you want to visually find a suitcase lying at its foot. In addition, you do it in dense fog," the journalistic duo Holly Yan and Ed Lavander bring us closer to the level of difficulty.[129] The search was disturbed by ocean currents, which scientists mapped using thermal imaging. Oceanographer David Griffin explained that the remains could

---

[128] „Malaysia Airlines MH370: submarine to be deployed as oil slick spotted." - https://www.telegraph.co.uk/news/worldnews/australiaandthepacific/australia/10764523/Malaysia-Airlines-MH370-submarine-to-be-deployed-as-oil-slick-spotted.html

[129] YAN, Holly – LAVANDERA, Ed: „How deep is deep? Imagining the MH370 search underwater". - https://edition.cnn.com/2014/04/10/world/asia/malaysia-airlines-ocean-depth/index.html

be located where two ocean currents pass each other and that it will therefore be very difficult to find them.[130]

However, the search was complicated by the relief of the seabed, which is minimally mapped there. There are underwater ditches and canyons 7,600 m deep in this body of water, as well as about 100,000 seamounts rising a kilometer and more above the sea bottom, and mostly unmarked.

31.18. The yellow submarine is heading to the depths

In mid-April 2014, searchers used the DSV Bluefin-21 underwater robot to search. This yellow, 5-meter torpedo-shaped submarine was designed to collect data to create a sonar map that would include any debris on the seabed, and if a positive discovery was made, to record the objects over an area of about 600 square kilometers after replacing the sonar with a camera. During the first dive on April 15, which had to be prematurely terminated, the submarine exceeded the depth limit of 4,500 meters and had to return.[131] The DSV Bluefin 21

---

[130] AMOS, Jonathan: "Malaysia Airlines MH370: Searching in an ocean of uncertainty." - https://www.bbc.com/news/science-environment-26956798

[131] „Missing flight MH370: Robotic sub first mission cut short". - https://www.bbc.com/news/world-asia-27030741

completed the dive in just six hours, although it was expected to spend twenty hours under water, sixteen of which, alone exploring the bottom.

In the following days, the DSV systematically surveyed the seabed until the operation was interrupted by a tropical JACK storm. Australian Prime Minister Tony Abbott at a press conference in Canberra announced that searchers in the indicated basin hadn't found any evidence of the Malaysian plane crash: "At the moment, it is unlikely that we will find the remains of the plane on the surface of the ocean. Already 52 days have passed since the disappearance of the flight MH-370. Most of the materials soaked up with water and sank. Therefore the search must go to the next phase."[132]

Following this statement, the naval operation went from visual search from ships and planes to viewing the ocean floor with sensor devices. After the DSV Bluefin 21 submarine had been mapping most of the ocean floor for two weeks, it was time for the crews of ships and search craft to systematically survey the entire body of water and the possible crash site, in the belt 700 km long and 80 km wide. "I want families, the whole world to know that Australia will not escape its

---

[132] „Missing plane: Search enters 'new phase'." - https://www.bbc.com/news/world-asia-27184295

responsibility. We will do everything humanly possible to solve this mystery," Prime Minister Abbott added at the end.

At the end of May 2014, the unpleasant truth that everyone had started to expect in the last days of the search came to light - the wreckage of the plane was not in this area, and subsequent searches had to focus on further data research and exploration of the seabed in other areas.[133] In late April, Australian company GeoResonance came out with another hypothesis about where the plane had gone missing, claiming that 190 kilometers off the coast of Bangladesh, material with traces of aluminum, titanium, copper and other elements derived from Boeing-777 was discovered. "Our company does not claim that it is the MH-370, but it should be examined," said Pavel Kursa, the company's director.[134] At the same time, GeoResonance started its own search on March 10, 2014, just two days after the plane had disappeared. The remains found in the new photos analyzed by the company's experts are not visible in the photos taken on March 5, before the loss of the plane.

Two Bangladesh frigates set off on May 5, 2014, five thousand kilometers from the original exploration area.

---

[133] „Malaysia missing MH370 plane: 'Ping area' ruled out." - https://www.bbc.com/news/world-asia-27615173

[134] „Malaysia missing MH370 plane: 'Ping area' ruled out." - https://www.bbc.com/news/world-asia-27615173

However, on-site verification yielded no results, neither did the analysis of strange debris washed ashore on the south coast of Western Australia, near Augusta. Local police seized and handed over to Perth investigators, metallic objects up to two and a half meters long, covered with laminate on one side and containing riveted joints. But these were not the remnants of the missing flight MH-370.[135]

31.19. Worse than on Mars

The Indian Ocean basin where flight MH-370 probably disappeared is one of the least explored corners of our planet. While scientists prepared a more detailed map, its accuracy was not very high, and with all due respect to their work, it cannot be forgiven that if the lost Boeing were to be searched directly on Mars, searchers would have a better topographic tool at hand.

Although it sounds paradoxical, thanks to satellite images, we know much more about the surface of the Red Planet which is 200 million kilometers away, than about most of the world's ocean beds. In the southern Indian Ocean region, the sonar

---

[135] „MH370 search: Investigators dismiss Australia debris." - https://www.bbc.com/news/world-asia-27124532

mapping of the sea relief took place in the 1960s, long before GPS was launched. The position of the ships was more complicated and not as accurate as it is today, as is the case with the measurement results recorded on graph paper.

To help locate flight MH-370, NOAA[136] experts Walter Smith and Karen Marks mapped an area of 1,400x2,000 kilometers. They used data streams from search vessel sonars, as well as data from satellites recording even small changes in sea level. To some extent, this has an impact on the morphology of the bottom and allows indirect reconstruction of its profile. Submarine mountain ranges create small gravity anomalies, so more water accumulates above them, creating local 'bulges' on the surface.

The accuracy of this map equals a quarter mile, but it was still useful for the searchers. The seabed profile is important for determining the direction of sea currents influencing the possible migration of the remains or fuselage of a lost aircraft, although echolines and sonars are still the best way to detect them at depths over half a kilometer. After all, the searchers in this area have failed, perhaps due to a lack of effort. According to Walter Smith and Karen Markx, comprehensive mapping of the ocean floor would take around two centuries, and cost hundreds of millions of dollars.[137]

---

[136] National Ocean and Atmospheric Authority

This is why Australian scientists gratefully took the opportunity in early June 2014 to record an unusual low-frequency sound captured by a couple of submarines in the Indian Ocean off the west coast of Australia during flight MH-370. Researchers at Curtin University of Technology in Perth analyzed the signal to find out if it was the sound of an airplane falling into the ocean.[138]

However, even here the "curse" of the missing Boeing-777 has arisen, ending in failure.

In June 2014, the Australian government hired a private Dutch company, Fugro Survey, for the largest and most expensive ocean exploration ever, after a prior selection process. $60 million was a fair price for exploring 60,000 square kilometers of ocean, the bottom of which lies about six kilometers below the surface. The oceanographic vessel RV Fugro Equator thus joined the Chinese vessel RV Chu Kche Chen and the American MV Go Phoenix, while the search fleet had robotic submarines with sonars and cameras.

---

[137] AMOS, Jonathan: „MH370 spur to 'better ocean mapping'." - https://www.bbc.com/news/science-environment-27589433

[138] O´CONNOR, Andrew: „MH370: Curtin University team checks undersea recorders for sounds of plane crash." - https://www.abc.net.au/news/2014-05-29/curtin-university-team-researches-mh370-sounds/5487054

At the same time, the search area was marked further south than before. This was done by re-analyzing satellite data on the movement of the missing plane. The redefined area of the "seventh arc" was delineated 1,500 kilometers south of Perth in the form of a narrow 60,000 square kilometer boomerang. The three-year search, however, didn't bring the expected results, although the Malaysian government hired the private company Ocean Infinity. "Despite all efforts, the best available scientific knowledge, cutting-edge technology, modeling and advice from highly qualified experts, the plane hasn't been located," officials from Australia, Malaysia and China said in a joint statement.[139]

31.20. Materialized ghost traces

At the end of June 2015, on the coast of the French Indian Ocean island of Réunion, seven hundred kilometers east of Madagascar, in the Saint Andre commune, two-meter-long metal artifact that looked like a flap from a Boeing-777 wing

---

[139] PERRY, Juliet – BERLINGER, Joshua – STERLING, Joe – BLOOM, Deborah: „MH370: Search suspended but future hunt for missing plane not ruled out." - https://edition.cnn.com/2017/01/17/asia/mh370-search-suspended/index.html

was found by the staff of a beach cleaning company. The French Civil Aviation Safety Authority, in collaboration with Malaysian and Australian colleagues, reported, inter alia, that on one side of the artifact was the BB670 number corresponding to the maintenance code, while an Air Australia flight engineer operating in Réunion reported to journalists that it was 657-BB. However, experts were so unanimous on the interpretation that Australian Prime Minister Warren Truss didn't hesitate to say that he was "almost certain" of its origin.[140] The ghost traces did materialize.

The next was air transport of the wing to France for further testing at the Ministry of Defense laboratory in Toulouse with the help of experts from Boeing and the Australian Transport Safety Authority. "The found part will be examined with the most modern means, especially with an electronic microscope. This way, we should recognize how the part has broken," said French expert Pierre Bascary.[141] "However, miracles cannot be

---

[140] O´ SULLIVAN, Matt: „MH370: Reverse modelling to determine final resting place 'almost impossible', says Warren Truss." - https://www.smh.com.au/business/companies/mh370-reverse-modelling-to-determine-final-resting-place-almost-impossible-says-warren-truss-20150731-giorwh.html

[141] „Experts meet in Paris over Boeing 777 debris". - https://www.thelocal.fr/20150803/experts-to-meet-in-france-over-boeing-777-debris

expected relying on this analysis," said his colleague Jean-Paul Troadec.

Yet some miracle happened. "It is almost certain that it's about the MH-370 flight, but relevant legal evidence is being sought," said Xavier Tytelman[142], French Aviation Security Specialist, on August 5, 2015. According to a statement by Malaysia's Transport Minister Liow Tiong Lai, during the inspection of the broken flap, inside it there was found a seal and records regarding the machine maintenance.[143] Thus, the issue of identification was satisfactorily resolved by checking the found serial number, production plans, material used, production process and chromatographic analysis of the color trace.

Experts also examined a piece of the trunk found near the remains, as a result of which it was found that it came from the missing plane. However, the same cannot be said of the other remains discovered on the coast of Réunion by its inhabitants. Their discovery, which was to be the plane's door discovered

---

[142] „MH370: les experts vont faire parler le fragment d'aile". - https://www.nouvelobs.com/monde/20150805.AFP5725/mh370-les-experts-vont-faire-parler-le-fragment-d-aile.amp

[143] SPYKERMAN, Neville – AHMAD, Zuhrin: Liow: „Maintenance seal on flaperon matches MAS records." - https://www.thestar.com.my/News/Nation/2015/08/06/Liow-flapperon-matches-MAS-records/

south of Saint Denis, was announced by BBC[144] on August 2, 2015. According to the British reporters, there were foreign inscriptions and probably logo on the object.

And here the story gets complicated. Azharuddin Abdul Rahman, the High Representative of the Malaysian Civil Aviation Authority, told the Associated Press that it was not an airplane door but a piece of a domestic aluminum ladder. At the same time, representatives of local authorities denied that they had considered other possible fragments of the aircraft. Will we believe it? On August 2, 2015, Sky News reported that some plane wreckage lay on the beach in a different location than the fragment that had already been examined by experts in France. The police put another piece into the sealed container, and declined to comment.[145]

The AFP photojournalist saw police officers picking up pieces of metal covered with Chinese characters that were attached to what looked like a handle.[146] British daily The Daily

---

[144] MH370 search: „New debris on Reunion investigated." - https://www.bbc.com/news/world-asia-33750811

[145] „MH370 Search: Metal Object 'From Ladder'." - https://news.sky.com/story/mh370-search-metal-object-from-ladder-10350637

[146] BENHAMIA, Mahdia – WOLF, Sonia: „No plane link to new debris in island hunt for MH370 clues." - https://news.yahoo.com/metallic-debris-found-la-reunion-island-

Telegraph, referring to local residents, wrote that there was possibility that the remains of the plane had been washed ashore on Réunion a quarter earlier, but no one had been aware of the missing flight MH-370. For example, Nicolas Ferrier claimed that he had found a blue seat on the beach in early May, which, like other finds, was burnt as garbage.[147]

Malaysia has asked the governments of the surrounding islands to help find more debris. The island of Mauritius, 225 km from Réunion, dispatched planes to monitor the basin, and Coast Guard units continued to search. This was also the case in Madagascar, Comoros, Seychelles and Maldives.[148]

The inhabitants of Réunion, who searched the shores of their island, also didn't disappoint. "People there are more careful. And many of them believe that any metal object found on the beach is a remnant of the MH-370 flight. However, the coast there is covered with objects and debris that the ocean is

legal-source-085646037.html?guccounter=1

[147] CHARLET, Dionne: „MH370 Investigation: Plane Seat Found Three Months Ago, Luggage Burned". -
https://www.inquisitr.com/2304916/mh370-investigation-plane-seat-found-3-months-ago-luggage-burned/#ixzz6BmtKVv83

[148] ALEXANDER, Harriet: „MH370: Malaysia calls for help in wreckage search near Reunion". -
https://www.telegraph.co.uk/news/worldnews/mh370/11778611/MH370-Police-urge-caution-amid-reports-of-washed-up-plane-door.html

constantly washing ashore," said Jean-Yves Sambimanan, spokesman for the city council of Sant-Andre in his speech on the glorious initiative of his countrymen.[149]

31.21. An unsuccessful search in sea currents

According to all data, some of the plane's debris was carried by sea currents 4000 km away from the probable crash site in the southeast part of the Indian Ocean, to the island of Réunion. However, scientists' opinions differed and still diverge on the possibility of finding further evidence. For example, oceanographer Roland Triadec said that Réunion is just a poppy seed lost in the Indian Ocean, and the likelihood of other debris being washed ashore on its beaches is low. However, his scientist colleague Vassen Kauppaymuthoo from neighboring Mauritius objected to him: "If the object found in Réunion is indeed part of the Malaysian plane that fell into the water in the Indian Ocean, other remains should also be discovered in the area."[150] His view was also supported by a

---

[149] „No Plane Link to New Debris in Island Hunt for MH370 Clues." - https://www.ndtv.com/world-news/no-plane-link-to-new-debris-in-island-hunt-for-mh370-clues-1203145

[150] MOONIEN, Vel: „«La zone du crash semble être située près des îles

mathematical model developed by the Australian research agency CSIRO, whose computer experts modeled data on ocean currents, wind speed and direction, and wave size.

Other findings soon confirmed the accuracy of these estimates. In the first week of August 2015, other objects most likely from the unfortunate flight MH-370 appeared on the coast of Réunion. According to Malaysian Prime Minister Najib Razak, seat covers and window components were found in the same location where waves had washed ashore the flap just a few days earlier. Interestingly, French authorities were reluctant to release information from the Kuala Lumpur government, while Australian searchers allowed the doubts to disappear entirely: "More materials was handed over to the police. They are under review but none of the objects appear to have come from the aircraft." If this conflicting information from Malaysian, Australian and French searchers is also misleading in today's deliberations, we can imagine what embarrassment they have prepared for the families and relatives of the missing passengers: "Why the hell some confirms it and others not?" asked Sara Weeks from Christchurch, who had a brother on board.[151]

Kerguelen», dit Vassen Kauppaymuthoo." - https://www.lexpress.mu/article/266478/zone-crash-semble-etre-situee-pres-iles-kerguelen-dit-vassen-kauppaymuthoo

[151] „MH370 search: Families vent anger over inquiry." -

Even this question remains unresolved to this day, although investigation regarding items aboard the missing Boeing continue.

In late February 2016, more debris was washed ashore on the coast of South Africa, and experts believe the two parts of the fuselage are most likely from the lost MH-370 flight. The dimensions, material used and construction fully corresponded to this. One of the objects is an almost one-meter-long piece of metal with a warning sign "Do not stand!"

"The analysis allows to conclude that it is almost certain that these are the remains from the flight MH-370," Australian Transport Minister Darren Chester said in a statement. According to him, the location of the find fully corresponds to the one where, according to the model's calculations, objects can be carried by the sea currents.[152]

Meanwhile, American lawyer Blaine Gibson discovered a wreckage off the coast of Mozambique during a private search and reported another finding of suspicious items from Nosy Boraha Island near Madagascar in June 2016. Photographs of handbags, Angry Birdz children's bag, Muslim prayer cap, empty electronics boxes that he posted on social networks,

---

https://www.bbc.com/news/world-asia-33801894

[152] „MH370 search: Mozambique debris 'almost certainly' from missing plane." - https://www.bbc.com/news/world-asia-35888405

again attracted the attention of the world, just as they aggravated the wounds of the victims' families. "They were located on the same 18 km stretch of beach where I found the plane wreck," he told a BBC journalist.[153] Gibson wasn't a member of the investigative team, but he devoted his free time and money. This decision prompted him to attend an event to commemorate the first anniversary of the tragedy, and since then he has conducted searches in the Maldives, Mauritius and Burma.

Considering the expertise of these fragments, the experts suggested that during the final phase of the flight, the unfortunate Boeing fell uncontrollably to the surface of the Indian Ocean. Meanwhile, Australian and Malaysian authorities reported that apparently none of the pilots had been in control of the plane. However, there were opinions that it was possible that the aircraft had landed in a controlled manner. A gliding, descending flight would perfectly explain why the debris was not discovered in previously identified search zones. Therefore, the conclusions of Australian investigators confirmed the hypothesis of the plane crash. "The flaps on the aircraft's wings were in flight position when they

---

[153] WESTCOTT, Richard: „MH370 search: Photos of possible personal items released". - https://www.bbc.com/news/world-asia-36571822

hit the surface. "The right flap was in a neutral position[154] at the time it probably broke off the wing," said a November 2016 report by Australian investigators.[155] Satellite contact with the plane confirms that the Boeing was descending rapidly before disappearing.

On March 8, 2019, on the fifth anniversary of the tragedy, Malaysian Transport Minister Anthony Loke announced that if anyone could convince him of the effectiveness of new technologies in discovering lost aircraft, he was open to resuming the search.[156] "We are more than willing to start another search," he said to reporters and relatives of MH-370 passengers, and aviation safety expert Philip Baum added: "I believe that the wreck will be discovered, and I will get to know the cause of the accident. But I'm not sure if this will happen in my lifetime."

---

[154] This means that the plane wasn't configured to land, and the ailerons, flaps and slots were in the flight position, not the landing one.

[155] PALAZZO, Chiara – ROTHWELL, James: „MH370 was flown into water 'deliberately', says senior crash expert." - https://www.telegraph.co.uk/news/2016/08/01/mh370-was-flown-into-water-crash-expert-says/

[156] MARIA, Anna: „Malaysia willing to re-open search for MH370 5 years after its disappearance." - http://theindependent.sg/malaysia-willing-to-re-open-search-for-mh370-5-years-after-its-disappearance/

The mystery of the missing Boeing 777 remains unsolved...

31.22. Summary: Chronology of the Search for the Missing Flight MH-370

March 24, 2014 - an unknown Malaysian airline plane crashed in a remote part of the Indian Ocean. This was announced by Prime Minister Nadjib Razak, who referred to a new analysis of data records from satellites. The crash site, however, remains unknown.

January 29, 2015 - the Malaysian Civil Aviation Authority officially recognized the disappearance of the plane as a disaster. This step made it possible to pay compensation to the families of the victims.

July 30, 2015 - on the shore of the French island of Réunion in the Indian Ocean, the sea washed ashore a part belonging to the missing Boeing-777. Aircraft experts viewed all the photos taken of this object, 2.5 m long. They stated that it could be a flaperon, a combination of aileron and a flap from the rear part of the wing.

October 13, 2015 - information appeared that the remains of the Malaysian plane appeared in the south of the Philippines - unconfirmed.

March 2, 2016 - part of the Boeing-777 wreck was washed ashore in Mozambique. It was probably part of the plane that disappeared without a trace during the flight from Malaysian Kuala Lumpur to the Chinese capital, Beijing.

March 16, 2016 - the fragment found on the island of Réunion in the Indian Ocean probably doesn't come from the missing flight MH-370. The said fragment was found on Réunion by Johnny Beque - the same man that on the island in July 2016 found part of the wing from the missing plane.

October 7, 2016 - the fragment of the wing found in Mauritius comes from the missing flight MH-370. This was confirmed by Malaysian and Australian authorities.

January 17, 2017 - Australian, Chinese and Malaysian crews searched for the remains of the plane. The action ended without success after 1046 days.

January 10, 2018 - Malaysian authorities and the American company Ocean Infinity signed an agreement to resume the search for the missing plane. A search vessel sent by Ocean Infinity entered the search zone on January 2, 2018, and then searched an area of 25,000 square kilometers north of the previous search basin.

May 29, 2018 - official search for the missing plane was finished. The search, which was to last until April, was extended twice, to May.

July 30, 2018 - Malaysian offices made public the information of an independent search team that the flight route had been consciously changed and that the aircraft had been flying for 7 hours after the loss of communication. The reasons for the disappearance of this plane have still not been established, but the possibility of a third force acting cannot be ruled out.

Collected and edited by Dr. Miloš Jesenský

Chapter 32

Rothschild's Chip and Captain X's Testimony

As time goes on, more and more authors develop the conspiratorial theory of a forced landing of the aircraft from flight MH-370, somewhere in the Indian Ocean, e.g. on Diego Garcia Island, where the US Air Force, Navy and Space Force bases are located. There was unconfirmed information that a group of talented software specialists from China was on board the missing Boeing-777, working for the private firm Freescale Semiconductor Ltd. in Texas. They were to develop a revolutionary 2 mm Kinesis KL-03 microchip enabling futuristic military and espionage operations. This chip will allow to construct fly-sized drones, spread chemical and biological toxic agents, and infiltrate electronics in a variety of devices, including civil and military vehicles. And most importantly: it could be implanted into the human body.

The makers of this chip: Wang Peidong, Chen Zhijun, Cheng Zhihong and Jing Li, who owned the patent, and had 20% of the shares each, were to travel from Kuala Lumpur to Beijing on flight MH-370. After declaring them dead, one hundred percent shareholder became Freescale, controlled by the investment group Blackstone Group Ltd. Partnership with capital of USD 200 billion. Its largest shareholder is the American financial magnate Nathaniel Rothschild.[157]

The rights to shares were transferred three days after the disappearance of the Malaysian plane. This opens the way to a conspiracy theory: Were computer specialists headed to Communist China to hand over this key technology? The editor-in-chief of Veterans Today, Gordon Duff, published information supporting his claim saying that it was not possible

---

[157] As for the MH-370, we would like to remind you that a similar situation took place in the case of the flight to Smolensk, where the main people of the country were on board one plane: the president, marshals, commanders of troops and parliamentarians ... It was exactly the same mistake that the Freescale bosses later made.

that the world powers hadn't known about the further fate of the missing plane:

We know that a Boeing 777-200 is a fly-by-wire aircraft with control mechanisms that enable the CIA "in case of emergency" to remotely control the aircraft. That such a design and implementation already exists, was confirmed by the Boeing Co., Raytheon Co. and some commercial pilots. The New York Times and other mainstream media reports of events during the flight of the MH-370 were imprecise and misleading. As soon as the Malaysia airline's MH-370 flight was announced missing, a massive covert search operation began. Nobody says anything about it, nothing has been written about it, and its scale is unknown to this day.[158]

In addition, Duff continues to say that what the world press reported about the loss and crash of the MH-370 is nonsense, and that in fact the flight was constantly monitored by the satellite system and the cooperating NORAD stations, using a secret device installed on board Boeing. And this is not a fantasy - as early as December 2006, a scientific journalist John Croft wrote about it on the pages of the "Flight Global" magazine:

---

[158] DUFF, Gordon: „Flight 370: The CIA Hoax." - https://www.veteranstodayarchives.com/2014/03/27/flight-370-the-cia-hoax-gordon-duff/

Boeing has obtained a US patent for a system that, when activated, takes away all the pilot's ability to control the aircraft and directs it to another destination. This "resistant" autopilot can also be activated by the pilots themselves when the on-board sensors break down, or CIA agents (or others) can take control of the plane if, for example, terrorists take control of the cockpit. Boeing says it constantly seeks and tests ways to improve the safety and efficiency of the world's air fleet.[159]

Let us recall that at the same time, already in 2006, Raytheon Corporation also received a contract to implement the "Advanced Route Evaluation System" (ARES) in cooperation with the already existing system under the supervision of the CIA.

There was also a testimony from one pilot, let's call him Captain X, who flies a Boeing-777, and he commented on this for "New Eastern Outlook":

It's a great, safe plane. Most systems have triple redundancy, so if one complete circuit breaks (and I don't mean just its part) there are usually two more on board to take on its role. It was designed with ease of use in mind, so that pilots from third countries could use it. Safety functions have also been built into

---

[159] CROFT, John: „Boeing autopilot would seize back control from hijackers". - https://www.flightglobal.com/boeing-autopilot-would-seize-back-control-from-hijackers/70937.article

the Malaysian aircraft. There are many communication systems on it: three VHF radios, two SatCom systems, two HF radio systems, plus transponders and real-time monitoring via CPLDC and ADS B with the use of SatCom, ACARS, VHF, and HF systems. Dispatchers always know where we are - they know our position, altitude, speed and so on. They also know what shows our dashboard. Big Brother sees everything! Only a few control devices cannot be disabled, one of which is the engine monitoring system. The Malaysian plane, like our 777, had Rolls Royce Trent engines. Rolls Royce rents out its engines to us and remotely monitors their activity. A few years ago, one of our Boeing-777s showed gradual oil leakage. This crash was not so serious as to raise a warning on the plane, but they had a problem with the Rolls Royce. It is based in England, so they contacted our agency which sent a message to the crew via SatCom to inform them about the Rolls Royce's request to closely monitor the oil pressure and temperature of the left engine. The crew behaved appropriately. The plane landed without any problems, but when it touched the ground, the left engine got turned off, which was caused by a replacement operating system that doesn't allow the engine to be turned off while the machine is in the air, but only on the ground. Decent technique. Most importantly, Rolls Royce monitors these engines 100% while they run.[160]

Proponents of the MH-370 conspiracy, therefore, believe that the plane was constantly monitored even after it "officially" disappeared from civilian radar screens. They claim that there were hidden systems on board that could take control of the plane and direct it to land. This view is not only the domain of authors shifting the fine line between fact and fiction. Sir Tim Clark, CEO of Emirates Airline, operating 127 Boeing-777s, who was very dissatisfied with the investigation into the incident said: "I believe that someone took control of the plane and maintained it until the very end."[161]

Dr. Miloš Jesenský

---

[160] „About the Malaysian airlines Boeing 777 that disappeared". - http://lorenzo-thinkingoutaloud.blogspot.com/2014/03/about-malaysian-airlines-boeing-777.html

[161] SPAETH, Andreas: „Emirates Head Critical of MH370 Investigation." - https://www.spiegel.de/international/business/mh370-emirates-head-has-doubts-about-investigation-a-996212.html

Chapter 33

Flight MH-370 on a blind track...

There is a writer in Polish fantasy who could face this puzzle. It is Stefan Grabiński (1887-1930), one of the most original authors of novels, short stories and horror stories, in the United States referred to as "the second Lovecraft" and "Polish Poe", today - unfairly - forgotten, as usual in our country, in which geniuses are not remembered and mediocrity is rewarded. In 1919, was published his anthology of short stories "Demon ruchu" (The Demon of motion), including a story that I associate with the events of March 8, 2014, titled "Ślepy tor" (Blind track), adapted by Ryszard Ber in 1967. The action of the piece is seemingly trivial. On the train to Groń, you meet several interesting figures from the world of science and public life - a total of 13 people who learn from the demonic Wiór Tracker that the train they are traveling on is redirected to the Blind Track, where it will crash. Indeed, the train in a mad rush passes the switch and continues to accelerate towards the final buffer, and ...there is a hellish crack like from shattering of carriages, furious rattle of iron being crushed, the thud of bars and buffers, clapping of raging wheels and chains. Amid the hustle and bustle of seemingly split benches, falling doors, amidst the rumble of collapsing roofs, floors and walls, among the clatter of bursting pipes, wires and tanks, the desperate whistle of the locomotive groaned... Suddenly everything fell silent, stuck to the ground, blown away, and the ears were filled with a great, powerful, infinite hum... And that humming duration wrapped the whole world for a long, long time, and it seemed that all earthly waterfalls were playing a menacing song, and that all earthly trees were rustling with their countless leaves... Then, it became deaf too and a great silence of darkness spread over the world. In the dead and dumb skies, stretched someone's invisible, very caressing hands, and stroked the soothing palls of space. And under this gentle caress, some soft waves wobbled, swam in silent runes and lulled to sleep... To a sweet, quiet sleep...

How lovecraftian that is, isn't it? Terror and poetry in one. Now look, Reader, does it not look like the plane crash that happened to the Malaysian Boeing-777? The same atmosphere - a carefree journey that turns into a horror, a nightmare for those who remained waiting for any sign from that side, from their loved ones ... This catastrophe, because there is no doubt that it was a catastrophe, brought with itself - as in Grabiński's story - a breeze of the Unknown. People think that some demonic forces were involved, which made travelers and crew disappear somewhere over the vastness of the Indian Ocean.

And here comes the second author, contemporary, Remigiusz Mróz, and his sensational religious horror entitled "Czarna Madonna" ("Black Madonna") (published by Czwarta Strona, Poznań 2017), in which one of the starting points is the disappearance of a powerful passenger, and the game revolves around parousia - the Second Coming of the Son of God to this world, which various demons and of course the head of Hell himself want to prevent... Mróz's horror is great. The author assumes that the hijacked planes will return, with Jesus Christ himself on one of them, and that the events described in the Apocalypse of St. John will happen. It all sounds very interesting, but this is just a horror film hatched in the author's imagination. Human nature is such that, once it has experienced the extraordinary, it wants every thing to be related to it, as count Jan Potocki wrote.[162] Whether in the

---

[162] Jan Potocki – „Rękopis znaleziony w Saragossie".

times of Potocki, Grabiński or Mróz - in the 19th, 20th and 21st centuries, people are curious, and curiosity is the first step to getting to know the Unknown. And it doesn't mean that we will know it...

Well, the MH-370 has not yet returned to either Malaysia or China. Its remains were most likely photographed by a French photo intelligence satellite over the Indian Ocean, somewhere between 100 and 105 degrees east longitude and 35 degrees south latitude, or about 920 km west of the nearest land - Cape Leuvin in Western Australia. All searches were made north of this point.

But let's not be glad, because the French satellite could photograph not the remains of the plane, but some plastic debris that was on the eastern edge of the Indian Ocean Vortex - a gigantic collection of plastic debris and waste that flowed there with currents from Africa, Asia and Australia. Four similar stains are found in oceanic vortexes in the Pacific and Atlantic. This is something similar to the Sargasso Sea, but instead of oxygen-rich algae, plastic debris floats there, which slowly decomposing, poison and suffocate sea creatures ... So it's not certain that these were the remains of the crashed Boeing-777 from flight MH-370.

Of course, the remains were found, but not in the ocean, but on the beaches of India, Sri Lanka, Mauritius, Réunion, Somalia, Kenya, Tanzania, Mozambique, and Madagascar. A total of 30 large fragments, by the end of 2018. The thesis is confirmed that the plane simply fell into the water from the altitude of 10,000-11,000 m, hitting it like a concrete slab. Lighter debris floated on the surface, carried by currents surrounding the Vortex, and the wreckage rests at the depth of five kilometers. It is enough to look at the Indian Ocean bottom relief in that area to realize the scale of the difficulty! The bottom is crisscrossed by ravines and crevices, and underwater mountains rise from it. Ocean ditches reach a depth of 22,550 ft/7,440 m. The search for such a small object as a plane wreck on this scale is like searching for a needle in a haystack. So far, all attempts to find the Malaysian Boeing have failed ... Maybe when we have the means to penetrate such depths, the wreckage of the Boeing-777 from the flight MH-370 will be found years later, like the wreck of the unfortunate Titanic... This is when its and the people's on board fate will be definitively determined and explained.

By the way, see, Reader, how much ambiguity, false information, erroneous data, sensational hypotheses and theories that have not been confirmed, guesswork and fruitless actions is in this matter. And this is all happening in the 21st century, where we could seem to track down a cockroach in any greasy spoon. And what could that mean? Well, that...

Flight MH-370 fell victim to some superpower secret service game, or to a genius madman - something à la the sinister

Professor Jimmy Moriarty, who wants a genius invention that he could use for his own purposes.

There is also a third possibility, namely - there is some Third Force behind the disappearance of the Malaysian plane, which may have wanted these people not to reach Beijing.

What was that? Correction of our Reality? - such as in the case of the Titanic disaster.

Or maybe of creating a turning point in our human history.

It might as well be the elimination of chronoclasm: on board this Boeing-777 was someone or something that was brought to us from the Future and had to be returned to that Future.

Or maybe it was some alien artifact, so dangerous that they sacrificed the health and lives of several hundred people to recover it? Who knows?

For now, we will only be doomed to guesswork, speculation and hypotheses of the kind mentioned above. Unfortunately, it will not be otherwise, until we find the wreckage of the plane from flight MH-370 ...

R.K.F. Leśniakiewicz

THE END

TABLE OF CONTENTS

www.ingramcontent.com/pod-product-compliance
Lightning Source LLC
Chambersburg PA
CBHW050332270326
41926CB00016B/3415